Turner On Ice

Claire Hunt

Outline

Lyvia Yule, realized that her new closest companion, Sharissa, implied the thing she had said about Lyvia having her very own mate, who knows where. However, in light of the fact that a pig flew over her head, doesn't mean they truly fly. All things considered, that is the thing that she thought until she saw him. He was hers, and she needed him, no she wanted him, in the most exceedingly awful manner. In case she didn't have him, and soon, she planned to freak out. She'd read what befalls a Fated Mate in case they don't mate, and she won't allow that to occur, nor are her companions. Whenever she has asserted her mate, then, at that point, they can happen with their lives... Who is she joking? Their lives are never going to be the equivalent again. What's more she wouldn't have it some other way. As yet managing plunge poos, they end up warding off horny Shifters, and becoming familiar with the impending conflict, and why they were united back, after so long. The Goddesses have an insane funny bone, and they discover that the hard, yet fun way.

Chapter 1

Lyvia Yule gazed upward from the book she was finding out about Shifters and their mates. It was something she had acquired from the Kraftman house. They have such countless books about their race. Her brain had been blown when she'd went along with them at their family supper the previous evening.

At the point when Dustin had declared that he and Sharissa were getting hitched, his siblings howled and giggled and let him know he was pussy whipped.

Their mom had quite recently said single word. "Why?"

Sharissa had quieted them by letting them know that her mate was doing it for her. What's more they'd be brilliant to take pointers from him, for their mates may likewise be Human who will have them pussy whipped so quick their heads will turn.

That had gotten a roar from the men, however not a solitary one of them had contended with her. Their eyes had illuminated at the possibility of having their own Fated Mate. Indeed, even Mrs. Kraftman had appeared to be invigorated. She dislike Humans, however in case they're clung to the family, she made a special case. What's more Lyvia could see the lady venerated Sharissa.

The clamor she'd heard a moment back returned once more. She put the book down on the foot stool and strolled to the entryway. She squeezed her car to the entryway and tuned in.

"Meew."

She gradually opened the entryway and peered down to observe a little orange and dark striped cat attempting it's hardest to scale the steps of her yard.

"You helpless thing," Lyvia murmured. She strolled outside and hung over to pet the little cat. "Where's your mom?"

"Yowl."

Lyvia looked into when she heard the mom kitty and grinned. "Here is your kitty, lovely mother." The mom feline looked actually like her little cat. "It's crisp over here; need to bring your infants inside where it's warm?"

The mom feline appeared to be limping, and Lyvia scowled. She gathered up the little cat then, at that point, strolled over to the mom, who gazed toward her cat in Lyvia's arms.

"Relax, I won't hurt that person," she said as should have been obvious, then, at that point, grinned. "Him."

"Howl." The mother feline limped as she scoured facing Lyvia's leg.

"Show me where your children are," Lyvia murmured as she watched the mother feline.

Since the time she was a young lady, she has had the option to some way or another, as it were, speak with family felines. Her mother had said it was the cat in her. Also perhaps she's right. However, in any case, the mom feline turned and limped towards a trench.

Lyvia's heart beat quick in her chest as she followed the mother feline. At the point when they got to the trench, she peered down and saw a splashed box on its side.

"Just cover you could find, huh, mom?" Lyvia murmured, following the feline down to the container.

Lyvia glimpsed inside, and her heart broke. "Gracious, mom. You were moving this one, right? What's more couldn't hold him any longer. That is the reason he went to my entryway, he had smelled my Tiger."

"Yowl." The mom feline said as though to say. 'No doubt, you got that right.'

"Alright, we should get you and this little man inside, then, at that point, tomorrow I'll have my companions assist me with covering your other little ones and give them a legitimate entombment."

"Whimper." The mom feline said, then, at that point, vanished into the container.

"Gracious, mom, I realize you need to bring your infants in general, yet we can't... "

"Yowl."

Lyvia moaned and got to her knees and investigated the case. "Goodness!" she said energetically when she saw a little cat moving. "There's another."

Lyvia came to in and snatched the cat. It was freezing cold, and Lyvia felt her heart skirt a thump. She hauled the cat out of the case and held it against her chest.

"We'll get you decent and hot very soon," she guaranteed.

The mom feline emerged from the container and gazed toward her.

"Come on, mother. We should get you and your infants out of the cool." Lyvia said, then, at that point, scooped the feline up into her arms and painstakingly made it up out of the trench and to her home without dropping any of them.

When she was inside, she set the mom feline down then searched for an unfilled box. She observed one to be that had accompanied her birthday present from her mom and collapsed in the folds then, at that point, set the little cats inside.

She observed her warming cushion and went it to the most minimal setting, then, at that point, lifted the little cats up and set the warming cushion inside. She got a little towel and set it over the warming cushion, then, at that point, put the cats inside the crate once more. She then, at that point, gotten the case and conveyed it over to the lounge chair and set it between the couch and end table.

"Here you go, mom," she said as she daintily tapped the crate.

The mom feline strolled over to the case, glimpsed inside, then, at that point, hopped in and began cleaning her little cats.

"Tomorrow after we burry your cats, I'm taking you to the vet and having you three investigated. Relax, I won't leave you there," she said cheerfully, then, at that point, strolled over to the entryway and opened it.

She expected to ensure there could have been no different survivors.

With a grimace, she returned to the container in the trench. She felt each cat and thought that they are totally frozen and not relaxing. With a weighty murmur, she strolled back to her home.

Out of eight cats, just two had endure the virus. How the mother feline had guarded them for this since a long time ago was a marvel. Yet, presently there's just two. Lyvia chose without further ado that she's keeping the mom and her Infants.

However, she wants to track down a legitimate name for her; she can't continue to call her mom.
"They are so cute," Sharissa spouted as she got the cat who had nearly kicked the bucket and snuggled it.

"She is Angel. Since she has a heavenly messenger," Lyvia said happily.

"So awesome," Sharissa said, nestling the cat.

"What's more this little man I named Tiger, obviously," Lyvia said with a smile.

"What did you name the mom?" Sharissa asked as she pet the mom feline.

"Symone."

"Pretty," Sharissa said happily.

"All things considered, the opening is burrowed," Dustin said as he went into the house.

Lyvia gazed toward her companion's mate and grinned. He was so tall and attractive; her companion is exceptionally fortunate.

"Much obliged," Lyvia said, "I like it."

Dustin shrugged, "it's dismal to see the honest pass on, and I was eager to assist."

Lyvia and Shar grinned at one another.

Shar assembled the two cats in her arms while Lyvia got their mom. Them three strolled to the trench, and Lyvia saw Dustin had even enveloped the little cats by a material and put them in the opening.

"What should we say?" Shar asked, watching her companion.

Lyvia shrugged. "Rest well, little ones?"

"Sufficient for me," Dustin said with a grin then, at that point, begun covering the opening with soil.

~□~

Sharissa and Dustin helped Lyvia take the mother feline and her cats to the vet.

Symone had something in her hip, and the vet had the option to eliminate it however in any case gave her a doctor's approval. Tiger and Angel were solid, and since Lyvia had saved them, they're warm and cheerful. A couple of meds for Symone and some perfect swathes and Lyvia had the option to take them home.

"I'm happy they're generally alright," Shar said as she nestled Angel.

Lyvia grinned at her companion. "I have an inclination you will bond with that little cat."

Shar grinned at her. "Would i be able to have her when she's weaned?"

Lyvia tapped her jaw as though she needed to consider it then, at that point, chuckled when Shar moped at her.

"Obviously you can. Three felines will be a great deal for me to deal with. Two will be sufficient difficulty, however basically I'll have organization."

"You will find your mate Lyvia. Simply stand by," Shar said happily.
Chapter 1
Lyvia abhors Mondays, particularly when she and her accomplice and dearest companion Sharissa Flemmings gets called into their supervisor's office.

"This task is screwed up," Mr. Trinkle said, highlighting his PC screen.

"Indeed sir," Sharissa said with a gesture. "We have fixed it a few times, yet somebody continues unfixing it."

Mr Trinkle grunted. "How are they unfixing your undertaking?"

"We don't have the foggiest idea. It simply continues to break," Lyvia said.

"Alright, so how about you fix the issue?"

Lyvia and Sharissa gazed at their chief.

"Mr Trinkle, as we said, we fixed it," Sharissa said, somewhat irritated.

"Somebody unfixed it," Lyvia said.

"I don't see the issue here, young ladies. Simply fix it once more," Mr. Trinkle said, then, at that point, waved for them to leave his office.

"The nerve of the man," Shar protested when they left their supervisor's office.

"How frequently have we fixed it?" Lyvia asked as they made a beeline for their work areas.

"Multiple times," Shar protested.

Lyvia gestured, "alright. Along these lines, we should fix it once again, and in the event that it's unfixed once more, we'll go to corporate."

Shar took a gander at her, her eyes wide, then, at that point, she burst into chuckling. "I truly like having you as my accomplice. My last accomplice would have prompted that we go through our time on earth fixing the issue, so we don't cause problems."

Lyvia laughed, "I see the reason why she didn't keep going long here."

Shar gestured.

"Indeed, we'll be there this time. Sheesh."

Shar looked into when she heard her mate's voice.

Lyvia grinned at her companion's thrilled face.

Dustin grinned when he saw them and went straight for Shar.

"Indeed, Raj, we will be there. Bye," he said with an aggravated snarl, then, at that point, hung up.

"Raj griping about us missing last week's down?" Shar asked as she folded her arms over his midChapter.

Dustin gestured and kissed her. "We better go above and beyond, he's at risk to drag us down there."

She laughed, "I'd prefer to see him attempt."

"Down where?" Lyvia asked, watching them.

"Dustin's companion Raj is a Professional Hockey Player," Shar said cheerfully.

"Heavenly fuck," Lyvia said, gazing toward Dustin. "Would i be able to come?"

"You like Hockey?" Shar inquired.

Lyvia gestured, "grew up with it. My father loves sports, particularly Hockey. Says it's the main spot a Shifter can release pressure and not go to prison."

Shar laughed, "never considered it that way. Anyway, I take it you like brutality?"

"Just on the ice," Lyvia said with a wide smile.

"Okay, you should come," Dustin said with a snort. "It will be great to have somebody who knows what's happening, so we don't get lost and consider the puck a ball."

Lyvia and Shar chuckled.

"Simply let me know what time and I'll be prepared," Lyvia said with a devilish smile.

~□~

"This spot is insane!" Sharissa yelled over the commotion when they entered the arena for Raj's Hockey game.

"I know!" Lyvia shouted back. "Isn't it incredible?!"

"I realize this isn't on the grounds that she's a Shifter!" Sharissa hollered to be heard over the group.

Dustin smiled, "obviously, your companion enjoys clearly and rambunctious."

Sharissa gestured, and Lyvia snickered.

"Shar, you don't need to holler; we would all be able to hear you without you yelling."

Sharissa and Lyvia turned in a circle until they tracked down the wellspring of the voice. The Kraftman siblings sat in the subsequent column, waving at them.

"Quiet down, Dylan, it's the energy of the spot," Sharissa protested.

They could hear every one of the four men laugh at her reaction.

"Come on, how about we snatch our seats," Livia said, then, at that point, grabbed hold of Sharissa's hand and strolled down the passageway, Dustin not far behind them.

"Hello sibling, happy to see you made it, at last," Daryl said as he watched Dustin and the young ladies plunk down in their seats in the column before the siblings.

"What? You're letting me know you came to last week's down?" Dustin asked, checking out his sibling.

His four siblings generally grunted simultaneously.

"We were here," Dylan said.

Sharissa laughed. "Apologies, young men. We... uh... had different things going on last end of the week."

"You mean like a wedding to design?" Dominic asked, fluttering his eyelashes at her.

Sharissa slapped his knee. "No."

"They were screwing," Dylan said with a chuckle and snort.

Others around them quieted down and took a gander at them. Shar's cheeks turned a radiant red.

"Let's assume it stronger, Dylan, don't think they heard you in Japan!" Dustin hollered with a snarl.

"Sorry," Dylan said with a laugh.

"Thus, you picked screwing your mate's minds out, over coming here, huh?" Daryl asked with a shake of his head.

Shar pivoted totally and hung over the rear of her seat, so she was nearer to the siblings.

"Dustin and I have chosen to begin our family, so we were... " She didn't get to complete her sentence.

Dylan and Dominic pulled her from her seat, and the four siblings embraced her with yells of fervor. Sharissa chuckled as every one of them kissed her on the cheek.

"Then, at that point, why are the screw you here?!" Dylan requested.

Shar laughed, and Dustin heaved.

"Brief you're scolding us for not being here, the following your hollering at us for being here. Make up your damn personalities." Dustin snarled at his siblings.

"All things considered, that was before we realized you were intending to give us a niece or nephew," Dominic said with a smile.

"If it's not too much trouble, ensure it's a nephew. We do not know how to manage a niece," Daryl said as he helped Shar back into her seat.

Shar grinned at him. "You realize we have zero influence over that. What's more, all you have to do with a niece is get her beautiful things."

Every one of the four men chuckled.
"Check out us, Sharissa. Do we look like men who purchase pretty things?" Drezden asked as he motioned to himself and his siblings.

"Who knows," Sharissa said with a wink, then, at that point, turned in her seat when the bell went off.

"This is so energizing," Lyvia said as she bounced all over in her seat.

"Here they come," Dustin said, highlighting the group that was coming out onto the ice.

"Whoopee, Raj!" Shar screeched as she leaped to her feet when she saw his number on the rear of a shirt.

Raj Cunningham turned a speedy turn and smiled when he saw his companions in the stands. He waved to them, then, at that point, turned around to the ice. Today is an exceptional game. Assuming they dominate this match, they're going to the end of the season games. Having his companions' help will make all that amount better when they wipe the ice with this group.

"Lovely fan you have there, Raj." Alec, his partner and companion, said, gazing toward the stands where Shar actually stood hooting his name. Alec was the main other Shifter in their group.

One more female voice mixed in with Shar's, one he didn't perceive. She should be the companion they had requested an additional a ticket for. Her voice sent delight up his spine, and he shook his head. Can't let a beautiful lady or voice occupy him this game.

"She's taken," Raj said, checking out his partner.

"The two of them?"

Raj shrugged, "not certain. The blondie is however, she's the mate of probably my dearest companion."

"Mate?" Alec asked, his eyebrows wrinkled.

Raj smiled, "better believe it. You recall the Kraftman siblings?"

Alec grunted, "better believe it, I recall them."

"Dustin tracked down his Fated Mate."

"Nothing of the sort," Alec protested.

"Gracious, yet there is. And every one of the narratives are valid."

"Every one of them?" Alec asked with splendid eyes.

Raj smiled, "each and every one of them."

The bell headed out to begin the game, and their psyches transformed from the potential outcomes of mates to the game.

"Good gracious! Your companion plays unpleasant!" Lyvia said energetically when Raj hammered a player from the other group against the glass across the ice for the fifth time.

"He does, doesn't he," Sharissa said with a chuckle.

"I love it!" Lyvia yelled with energy.

The ringer went off, calling the primary recess, and Shar took a gander at Dustin.

"I must pee."

Dustin laughed, "OK, darling."

"I'll go with you," Lyvia said as she got to her feet. "We can grab a bite and some brew before we return."

"Get us a brew as well," Daryl said as he gave Lyvia a fifty.

Lyvia grunted, "I'm keeping the change assuming I'm late getting back."

Daryl snickered, "bargain."

Dustin gave Shar some cash then, at that point, kissed her before he let go of her hand.

"Good gracious. See that line," Sharissa said with a moan.

Lyvia moaned, "we're never leaving."

"We will miss the beginning of the subsequent half," Shar said, bobbing all over.

"I have a thought," Lyvia said, grabbing hold of Shar's hand and pushing past the ladies. "Pregnant woman with a blasting bladder coming through," she said as she pushed individuals out of her way.

"Hello!" a lady shouted, giving Shar a push.

Lyvia turned on the lady and snarled at her.

The lady saw her silver eyes, and her face withered.

"I said, pregnant lady, coming through. Do you truly need me to let everybody know that you pushed a pregnant lady, since you were unable to hold back to take a crap?"

The lady's eyes messed with off of her mind as she checked out Shar. "Please accept my apologies," she murmured.

Lyvia smiled. "That is better," she said, then, at that point, transformed and maneuvered Shar into the following void slow down.

The two ladies broke into attacks of snickers.

After five minutes, they were in line for rewards.

"We can't utilize a similar stunt here," Sharissa said with a chuckle.

Lyvia snorted, "basically I'll be thirty bucks more extravagant."

Shar chuckled, "indeed, how about we check out the splendid side of things."

They at last got to the front and requested, then, at that point, stacked the plate and made a beeline for the stands. They were five minutes late, and the groups were at that point on the ice.

"Quit messing around, Raj!" Dustin howled as he stood up, waving his clench hand at his companion.

"Here you go," Shar said cheerfully as she gave him their plate.

"Much obliged, angel," Dustin said, then, at that point, sat back in his seat.

Lyvia was so captivated by the thing was occurring on the ice that she didn't hear the siblings requesting their lager. She saw Raj's number on the rear of one of the shirts and watched in interest as he hammered a similar man against the glass across the ice from them. Her eyes were stuck to him, and she was unable to pull away.

"Lyvia?!" Shar called out, however Lyvia didn't hear her.

Raj and a similar man skated on the ice towards her, and her heart beat in her ears. The man pummeled Raj into the glass directly before Lyvia, and she bounced. At the point when Raj saw her, time froze. She dropped the plate of brews and didn't hear the Kraftman siblings' shouts of fury.

"Oh dear," Shar said as she watched her companion and Raj, "I recollect that look."

Dustin watched the two then, at that point, laughed. "They're in a bad way.

"Mine," Lyvia ended up saying simultaneously as Raj.

Lyvia felt her Tiger murmur as they gazed at their mate.

Raj hammered his clench hand against the glass and got down on something she was unable to comprehend.

"What the heck?" Dominic muttered as he watched the two gaze at one another.

"Another match," Sharissa said cheerfully.

"In perhaps their greatest game?" Daryl asked with a snicker. "He's definitely screwed."

Raj kept on gazing at the delightful Shifter. His mate. He never suspected he'd at any point track down her. She looked similarly ravenous for him as he was for her.

"Come on, Raj, quit playing with the rabbit and get your head back in the game," a colleague hollered.

Raj snarled, "she isn't a puck rabbit. She's a companion of a companion, and she turns out to be mine."

The man grunted, "all things considered, I couldn't care less on the off chance that she's the Queen of Sheba. Get your head back in the game."

His mate strolled down the steps toward him. His eyes never left hers as she set her hand to the glass, where his hand was as yet squeezed against the opposite side.

"I will make you mine!" he snarled at her.

She grinned at him, and he knew there would have been a ton of fucking in their future.

"Cunningham!" his mentor roared.

Raj left his mate and got back to the game, yet his musings were never a long way from her.

Chapter 2

"Here's one that didn't break!" Dylan got down on when he tracked down a safe jug of bear.

"Give me that," Daryl said, grabbing the container of brew from his sibling.

"Hello, I tracked down that." Dylan heaved.

"Furthermore I'm the one out twenty bucks," Daryl said with a snarl.

"Fifty!" Dominic yelled with a snicker. "She will keep the change since she missed the beginning of the subsequent half."

Daryl snorted, "she dropped my lager; she should give me my change."

"She tracked down her mate," Sharissa said as she went to her siblings, "you can't blame her for that."

Daryl grunted, "I surmise not. Be that as it may, this brew is mine," he said, then, at that point, popped the cap and took a long swig from it.

Shar snickered, then, at that point, took their three brews and gave them to the next three.

"Hello!" Dustin snarled. "No, parting with my lager, lady."

Shar grinned at him. "In case you share your brew, I'll let you do that thing you like this evening."

Daryl spat a mouth brimming with brew all around his legs and began stifling.

The others giggled at Daryl.

Dustin's eyebrow shot up, then, at that point, he smiled. "Partake in the lagers, siblings," he said, then, at that point, winked at Shar.

"I don't believe they will come to the furthest limit of the game," Dustin said, highlighting Lyvia, who was pacing before the glass.

"They certainly won't make it home," Sharissa said with a gesture.

Raj hammered somebody against the glass before Lyvia, and she raced to the space he was at and squeezed herself against the glass.

"Individuals will believe she's a prostitute," Dominic said, watching Lyvia and Raj.

"She resembles a Tiger in heat," Drezden said.

"She essentially is," Sharissa said, watching her companion.

"You didn't behave like that when you met Dustin," Dominic said, watching Lyvia.

"Shar isn't a Shifter," Dustin said, grabbing hold of his mate's hand. "I sure behaved like them possibly more terrible," he said with a smile.

A noisy beat on the glass had everybody in the space hopping in their seats. Raj was attempting to break the glass to get to Lyvia. He presumably would have hopped up onto the glass assuming he wasn't wearing ice skates.

"Raj!" Dustin yelled as he leaped to his feet. "Keep your head in the game and your dick in your jeans. We'll carry her to you whenever you've cleaned the ice with the other group's heads!"

Raj's head jolted up to Dustin, then, at that point, he growled and skated away.

"Try not to believe that will keep going long," Shar murmured as she watched the Tiger Shifter skate towards his colleagues.

"Check out her," Dylan said, pointing at Lyvia, who was pacing before the glass once more, snarling.

"She resembles a confined creature," Shar murmured.

"She's not sane, that is without a doubt," Daryl said, watching Lyvia walk forward and backward. Every so often she would beat on the glass.

"For what reason wouldn't they be able to have met at a grill or our place?" Shar asked with a substantial moan.

"Fate is a bitch!" Dylan yelled.

"So be it!" Dominic shouted as he beat on his chest.

"I think everybody is going crazy," Shar murmured to her mate.

"It's the pheromones Lyvia is delivering into the air," Dustin said as he pulled her against him. "It's what happens when a female Shifter tracks down her mate and goes into heat."

"However, you're not behaving like a nut," she said as she investigated her shoulder at their siblings.

Dustin laughed. "That is on the grounds that I have my mate," he said then kissed her cheek. "Try not to misunderstand me I am horny as damnation and need to screw you at this very moment. Yet, I have more control then these yahoos. Furthermore I realize our companions need me with my head clear."

"Do we need to stress that some other Shifter will attempt to mate with her?" Shar asked, watching her companion. "Like with me."

"Ok fuck," Dustin snorted.

"How about we go have her covered," Shar said.

Dustin gestured, and they stood.

"Try not to contact me!" Lyvia shouted.

Shar checked out her companion. "Get the hellfire off her, you crossbreed," she shouted out as she got around the bar isolating the glass from the seats and seized the one who was pawing her companion. "Track down your own mate!" she shrieked, then, at that point, tossed the man over the rail and mostly up the steps.

"That is my mate," Dustin said gladly as he pointed at Sharissa.

"Shar," Lyvia murmured, "I can't take this any longer. I really want him like at this point."

Shar gestured as she clutched her companion. "Before long, Lyvia, soon."

Lyvia shouted a snarl, and Raj reacted.

"Poo, this glass won't keep them separated significantly longer," Dustin said, going along with them.

"Then, at that point, we'll eliminate Lyvia from his view... " Shar began to say.

Dustin in a split second shook his head. "Raj will go crazy looking for her."

Shar snarled when a man moved toward them.

"Allow me to relieve her hurt," the Shifter argued.

"Get the damnation out of here!" Shar shouted.

"See, Human... "

Dustin utilized his clench hand to quietness the ass before he said something inept regarding his mate. "I'll go converse with Raj; I will be right back," he said, then, at that point, pushed his direction to where Raj was situated in the break box standing by to be delivered back out onto the ice. "Raj!" he roared as he hit the glass behind his companion.

Raj went to Dustin, his silver eyes wild.

"Keep your head in the game, the sooner you win, the sooner you can guarantee your mate."

Raj's eyes appeared to clear a bit, and he gestured then gazed toward the clock. When the clock ran down, he bounced back out onto the ice and skated like he'd never skated.

Dustin grinned. Ideally, he'll remember that and beat down the other group. Raj could never pardon himself in the event that he let his group down as a result of his Shifter chemicals.

Dustin got back to his mate and Lyvia. There were two additional oblivious men in the walkway, and his siblings were waiting around the two clustered ladies.

"How's Raj?" Daryl asked, checking out Dustin.

Dustin gestured, "he may endure the game without killing somebody."

Dylan growled, "on the off chance that these damn Shifters don't let Lyvia and Shar be, I'm killing somebody."

"What are they doing to Shar? She is as of now asserted," Dustin asked, watching his mate.

"She's as yet a Fated Mate," Daryl said. "Furthermore with Lyvia letting off all that pheromone, they can smell Shar as well, asserted or not."

"Ok, fuck," Dustin snarled.

"It's OK, sibling," Dominic said, praising Dustin. "She has her siblings to secure her."

Dustin gestured. "Much obliged, Bro."

A signal went off, and they gazed toward the clock.

"Fifteen additional minutes of this insane ass poop," Daryl said.

"Mine," Lyvia said with a snarl when Raj skated out to the center of the arena.

"He is," Shar said as she clutched her companion, "and soon you can guarantee him."

Lyvia inclined toward Shar and murmured.

"Alright, that is new," Shar said with a giggle.

"It's her Tiger," Dustin said happily, "she remembers you as a companion."

"What's more an individual Fated Mate," Daryl said.

Shar gestured, "that's right, that is the thing that we are."

"Possibly you should begin The Fated Mates Club," Dylan said with a giggle.

Shar grinned at him. "Possibly, I will."

"Mother lover!" Dustin snarled when the ringer went off once more.

"What?" Shar asked, then, at that point, gazed toward the board with a moan. "Gracious, no."

"They're tied, and presently they're going into extra time," Dustin said with a snarl.

"The Goddesses really have a terrible awareness of what's actually funny," Daryl said as he ventured to the side to impede one more poop chute purpose on taking one of the people for himself.

"Raj, make the damn objective so you can guarantee your mate!" Dustin thundered.

Raj investigated at his mate and companions. They were shielding his mate from different Shifters, ensuring he gets his lady. He grinned and figured he could essentially do what Dustin inquired.

He turned around to the game and steered to the left when the man steered to the right. At the point when he saw the opening, rather than taking it, he pushed the puck over to Alec, who turned in an ideal circle with the puck to stay away from the poop chutes descending on him.

Raj could see that the pheromones his mate was setting off were influencing his partner, yet Alec's cerebrum was completely centered around the game. In contrast to Raj, who can scarcely imagine everything except his mate. Poo, he doesn't have the foggiest idea about her name.

"Presently, Raj!" he heard Dustin holler.

"Alec," Raj murmured.

Alec heard him, and he had additionally crowd Dustin. He pushed the puck to Raj, and Raj made the triumphant shot.

Dustin and his party cheered when Raj made the triumphant shot. Lyvia was so out of it she didn't see that her mate had dominated them the match.

"We want to get her to the storage space," Sharissa said, then, at that point, driven Lyvia away from the glass.

The Kraftman siblings framed a hindrance around the two ladies as they strolled up the walkway towards the storage space.

"How might we keep the remainder of the group out of there?" Daryl asked as they strolled down the huge corridor towards the storage spaces.

"Call Tate," Shar said as she saw her mate.

Dustin smiled at her. "My splendid mate," he said, then, at that point, taken out his telephone.

"Should we get Raj?" Dylan inquired.

"Trust me, he's now in there hanging tight for her," Dustin said with a snicker, then, at that point, gone to his telephone when Tate replied. "Hello mate, recollect that favor you owe me for attempting to turn my mate against me?"

"Man, I didn't, and I don't owe you poop. I dealt with Vega for you."

Dustin laughed, "OK, all good. Then, at that point, I'll owe you some help, a huge one."

"What's happening?" Tate asked, interested.

Dustin let Tate know what occurred and what they need from him and the Vampire burst into giggling.

"Alright, I will be there in a short time," he said, then, at that point, hung up.

"He's coming," Dustin said happily.

"Lyvia," Shar said as she constrained her companion to check out her.

Lyvia checked out her companion and grinned. "You were correct, Shar. I do have a Fated Mate."

Shar laughed, "indeed, and he's sitting tight for you in there. We will hold anybody back from strolling in on you. However, we can't remain here every night. Do you get it?"

Lyvia gestured. "My mate is in there?"

"Indeed," Shar said cheerfully.

"OK," Lyvia said, then, at that point, gone into the storage space.

Shar went to the others. "Presently, we ensure nobody interferes with them."

~□~

Lyvia took a full breath and strolled through the storage space. Her heart was hammering out of her chest, and her noses were erupting. She could smell him, and her tiger realized he was close.

She strolled around the bend toward the finish of the column and froze when she saw him. He was bare, and his body was great. It flickered in the light, and he has such countless great muscles. She truly adores the build of a Shifter. Also obviously, pigs do fly.

Raj twirled around when he felt her behind him. He had smelt her the moment she'd went into the storage space.

"You have too many garments on," he said, then, at that point, intellectually slapped himself.

Method for going, Romeo.

She giggled, "sorry, I was simply partaking in your... " She found him and down, and he knew precisely the thing she'd been getting a charge out of.

"Come here," he said as he spread his arms open.

She smiled, then, at that point, hurried to him and bounced on him.

He chuckled as they tumbled to the floor, her on top of him.

"We want to rush," she said, then, at that point, kissed his skin. "Shar and Dustin and the other Kraftman siblings are monitoring the entryway. They even brought in the Vampire."

Raj giggled. It's in every case great to have companions like them.

"All things considered, then, at that point, how about we get everything rolling... "

"Quiet down," she said with a snarl.

He didn't say any longer. Before he realized what was going on, Lyvia was exposed and sitting on his stomach, her trickling wet pussy spilling on his skin.

"Fuck!" he shouted out, then, at that point, turned her under him and entered her so quickly the delight detonated through his body.

She shouted, and he halted.

"Damn it," he protested.

He ought to have realized she was a virgin; Shifter females don't have intercourse with just anybody.

Chapter 3

"Try not to stop," Lyvia said, watching the feelings play across his face.

"I ought to have… "

"You did precisely what we are intended to do. Presently screw me!"

She heard his Tiger snarl, and their bodies moved as one.

"So great," Raj said with a moan. Who'd at any point figured he would track down his mate?

She's ideal. Lovely and a Tiger like him. Fuck, he wouldn't really mind assuming that she was a primate.

He stopped in his considerations, are there Baboon Shifters out there?

"Where has your brain gone?" his mate inquired.

He took a gander at her and grinned, then, at that point, let her know he thinking.

She chuckled, "not something I would think you'd ponder while fucking your mate interestingly. However, thank you for thinking me excellent and not mindful assuming I was a mandrill."

He smiled, "I currently like you. I figure we will get along extraordinary."

She grunted, "I trust so. Since there will be no other person for me."

He kissed her interestingly, and his cerebrum detonated.

"Good gracious," Lyvia groaned against his mouth.

Everything shivered, and the aggravation had just been there for under a moment. Presently, it was unadulterated joy.

His tongue contacted hers, and she felt her psyche liquefy. She was unable to consider everything except his kiss, his cockerel inside her, and the manner in which his skin felt against hers.

"So delightful," he murmured against her lips.

She murmured, "you're not downright terrible yourself."

He laughed, "I saw the manner in which you were taking a gander at me."

She snickered.

He moved to sit up, and a sensation neither of them had at any point felt before shook through their bodies.

"Blessed fuck," Lyvia groaned.

"Definitely," he said winded.

She groaned when he folded her legs over his hips and got to his feet. He hammered her back against the storage spaces and began fucking her so hard she was shouting out. Sensations developed then detonated, taking her to an entirely different universe of delight.

"Screw yes," Raj moaned as he banged into her, immovable.

He doesn't have the foggiest idea about his mate's name. How might he call it out when he spills his seed inside her?

"What's your name?" he asked as he covered his face in her neck.

"Lyvia," she said with a substantial gasp.

"Lyvia," he murmured, chills running down his spine, "I'm Raj."

She grinned, "I know."

He laughed, "obviously you do."

Lyvia screeched when he pulled out of her and set her on her feet. The devilish examine his eyes had her amped up for what he would do straightaway. He turned her, so she confronted the storage spaces then, at that point, pushed down on her back until she was twisted around. He entered her, and she shouted out his name.

"Blessed fucking crap!" he shouted out as he screwed her from behind.

"Have you perused any books on Fated Mates?" she asked as she grasped her tits to hold them back from insulting her.

"Definitely," he said as he hung over her back and slid his give over to her hill and effortlessly tracked down her clit.

"Oooohh," she groaned as sensations detonated through her body.

"I've been perusing them with the Kraftman siblings since we were fledglings."

"Right," she said with a groan. She'd failed to remember that Raj is companions with the siblings.

"Fuck! I'm going to cum," he said, then, at that point, unexpectedly, her front was squeezed against the storage spaces, and his lower arms were against hers, their fingers bound together.

"Blessed fuck!" she shouted out as a climax detonated through her body.

At the point when her pussy fixed around his chicken, he called out to out her, and his seed delivered somewhere inside her. She felt the bunch structure at her entry, yet that wasn't what had her consideration. Her wrists were consuming and felt like somebody had set them ablaze.

She shouted as the aggravation burned through her body. He shouted out and laid his temple against her shoulder. She kept on shouting as the aggravation kept on burning-through her.

"It said nothing in the books regarding this," Raj said with a snarl.

Her aggravation was harming him more than his own. He preferred not to hear his mate in such a lot of agony. His Tiger snarled and whimpered as the aggravation proceeded, and their mate shouted.

At last, the agony died down, and a bizarre inclination moved through his body. Like he was getting more grounded.

"Gracious," she murmured. "It's valid," she said with a murmur, "our association reinforces us."

He kissed her shoulder. "Basically we will not need to go through that singing aggravation once more."

She gestured.

"So," he said as he nipped at her shoulder. "Dustin said it requires around thirty minutes for the bunch to relax. Possibly we can utilize that chance to get to know one another."

She laughed, "sounds better compared to remaining here peacefully."
Shar recoiled when she heard Lyvia's shouts.

"What the heck is he doing to her?" Tate asked, gazing at the way to the storage space.

"It's the holding custom," Dustin said as he pulled Shar against his chest.

"Seems as though he's killing her," Tate said.

Shar shook her head as a chill ran down her spine. "It seems like somebody is consuming your tissue," she said, seeing her own markings.

"However at that point it seems like you're the most remarkable being in creation," Dustin said then kissed Shar's wrists.

"So essentially, the Goddesses brand you," Tate said as he checked out Shar's wrists.

Shar gazed upward into her mate's eyes. "We sort of considered it that way as well. They do look like brandings."

Dustin gestured, "possibly it's the Goddesses' method of marking their manifestations."

"The shouting has halted," Dylan said as he inclined his head against the divider opposite the entryway.

"Thirty minutes and they'll be all set," Dustin said, checking the time.

~□~

Lyvia felt the bunch mellow and moaned. The bunch didn't do any harm; it was simply awkward while remaining there essentially on her unstable toes.

"Need to allow our Tigers to have some good times?" he murmured into her ear.

Lyvia checked out him behind her, and her Tiger murmured. "For hell's sake, yes."

Raj smiled.

"Have you done this previously?" she asked, not certain assuming she needed to know the appropriate response.

He shook his head. "Our monsters just mate with their actual mate."

"Right," she said with a gesture. She hadn't gotten that far into her perusing, yet.

"Prepared?" he asked, then, at that point, kissed her shoulder.

"Is it accurate to say that you will take out first?"

He laughed, "not a chance. We're doing this now," he said, then, at that point, begun to move.

With a wild snarl, she let her Tiger dominate. She tumbled to every one of the fours, Raj still inside her from behind.

~□~

"It has been thirty minutes since the shouting halted," Dustin said, checking the time once more.

"I hear snarls and snorts," Tate said as he squeezed his ear to the entryway.

"Get back, you distort," Dustin said then opened the entryway.

They strolled down to the furthest limit of the walkway and halted when they saw two Tigers grinding away.

"Also you considered me a degenerate!" Tate said with a giggle, then, at that point, turned and left the storage space.

"They're delightful," Shar said, her cheeks dark red. She could swear she heard the Tigers chuckling, and Raj didn't stop...

"OK, it's an ideal opportunity to go," Dustin said, then, at that point, grabbed hold of her shoulders and diverted her from the mating Tigers. "You folks have 60 minutes, and we're hauling you out of here whether or not you're tied!" Dustin called out as they left the storage space.

"That wasn't something I needed to see this evening," Daryl said as he paced the corridor outside the storage space.

"They're fortunate," Dylan said happily, then, at that point, checked out Shar and Dustin. "Much more fortunate than both of you."

"In what capacity?" Shar inquired.

"Since they're the two Shifters and similar types of Shifter. They can fuck in their monster structures," Dylan said with a profound murmur.

Shar glared.

Dustin kissed her cheek. "Try not to pay attention to his ineptitude," he murmured in her ear, "you and I are comparably fortunate."

She gestured yet didn't feel as fortunate as she had before Dylan called attention to the slight issue to her. She's not a Shifter.

"Idiotic dipshit," Tate said as he slapped Dylan directly in the face.

"Damn it, Vampire, what the hell?" Dylan snarled as he put his hand to the rear of his head.

"You just caused your sister to feel to a lesser extent a mate since she's not a Shifter," Tate said with a snarl.

Dylan gazed at Shar with wide eyes. "Please accept my apologies, Seliana. I didn't mean it like that."

She shrugged, "it's alright."

"No, it's not," Dustin said with a snarl. "I trust when you track down your mate, she's a Human, then, at that point, we'll see where you stand," he said, frowning at his sibling.

Dylan's eyes extended then mellowed. "I'd be pleased to have a Human mate," he said then checked out Shar. "Assuming she's in any way similar to you, that is."

Shar laughed, "your mate will be her own individual. What's more you will adore her in any case."

Dylan laughed, "you're correct."

~☐~

"Hello everybody," Lyvia said happily as she and Raj left the storage space to observe their companions sitting tight for them.

"Good gracious," Shar said as she flung herself at Lyvia.

Lyvia snickered, "I wasn't gone above and beyond."

Shar laughed, "no, I'm glad that you tracked down your mate."

Lyvia grinned up at her mate. "So am I."

Raj smiled and set his arm over Lyvia's shoulders.

"It was proposed to me that I should begin The Fated Mates Club," Shar said, poking Lyvia. "You ready?"

Lyvia snickered. It really seemed like a smart thought. "Of course, we can get together double a week and talk about our mates."

"Precisely," Shar said with a chuckle.

"I just considered something," Dylan said, watching the two new Fated Mates.

"What?" Lyvia asked, watching her companion look at her new markings.

"Destined Mates can't be isolated for extremely long, or they can go crazy with need," Dylan said.
Everybody halted and gazed at him.

"Which book did you read that in?" Dustin inquired.

"Destined Mates and the Bonding," Dylan said.

"Right, I read something to that effect," Daryl said with a gesture. "The holding must be something standard, or the mates can lose themselves."

"Then, at that point, we've been doing it right," Dustin said with a smile.

"Eeww not a dream I really wanted," Tate said with a constrained gag.

"Quiet down," Shar said as she gave the Vampire a push. In her most out of this world fantasies, she'd never suspected she'd push a Vampire. "We're attempting to begin our family."

Tate smiled at her. "You can quit attempting."

"Not good," she said with a mope.

Dustin halted at his companions' words. "Tate?"

Lyvia's mouth dropped open. "Shar!" she shouted out as she pulled away from Raj and assaulted her companion.

"What?" Shar inquired. "I'm not sure why you're all seeing me like that."

"Shar, Mafilia," Dustin said as he pulled his mate from Lyvia's arms.

He can scarcely accept what his companion was saying. However, in the event that Tate has detected something. He gazed toward his companion. The Vampire gestured, and Dustin burst into tears. What the heck? He doesn't cry!

"What's happening?" Shar asked, gazing at Dustin.

"Shar, you're now conveying my whelp," Dustin said then kissed her.

"I trust you're not playing a joke here, Vampire," Daryl said with a snarl.

Tate smiled, "she's a little more than seven days pregnant."

"That is the point at which I quit taking my pill," Shar said with a screech.

Dustin laughed. Their first season of having intercourse with her off the pill had made a daily existence.

"Twelve additional weeks," Lyvia said with energy.

"Do you think we began our own as well?" Raj asked as he pulled Lyvia against him.

"Goodness God," she said as she gazed toward her mate, "I hadn't thought about that."

"Tate?" Raj asked, checking out the Vampire.

"What am I, the whelp master?" Tate protested, then, at that point, strolled over to Lyvia and sniffed at her neck. "No, not yet, Raj."

Lyvia murmured with alleviation.

Raj saw his mate. "Would you like to have my fledgling?"

She checked out him and shook her head. "Goodness, I do. In any case, I expected to get to know you first."

He grinned at her. "What about we start with me taking you to supper tomorrow evening?"

She gestured, "indeed, I might want that."

"Stand by a moment. What did you mean by twelve additional weeks?" Shar inquired. "Don't you mean nine additional months?"

Everybody took a gander at her.

"Sharissa, Mafilia," Dustin said, holding her nearby, "Shifters are just pregnant for thirteen weeks."

Shar's eyes messed with out. "Be that as it may, I'm Human."

"Doesn't make any difference," Tate said happily, "you're conveying a whelp, not a child," he reminded her.

"Twelve additional weeks, and you'll be a mom."

Chapter 4

"I can't completely accept that nobody saw I wasn't at the party." Raj said as he, his companions, and their mates lounged around in Dustan and Sharissa's home.

"That is the extraordinary thing about having a Vampire for a companion," Dustin said happily.

"You both owe me for this," Tate said, then, at that point, took a taste of his scotch on the rocks.

"We didn't complete the process of talking about what those two will do when Raj needs to go to his next away game," Dylan said, pointing among Raj and Lyvia.

"I can converse with Mr. Trinkle and concoct a task she can do from home," Shar said.

"I can't allow you to do that," Lyvia said with a grimace.

"Trinkle might be an asshat, yet I've worked under him for quite a long time. I know what he enjoys, and I can play at his inner self," Shar said cheerfully.

"That is really a smart thought. Assuming Lyvia can telecommute and email you her work, then, at that point, she can go with Raj and the group," Dylan said with a gesture.

"What's more how might we get her on the transport?" Dominic asked his sibling.

Everybody checked out Tate.

"What the hell?" Tate said, watching his companions. "Have I turned into the neighborhood trance inducer?"

"We could utilize your assistance once more, Tate," Dustin said. "Except if you need them to go crazy and most likely kill us all in our rest."

Tate grunted, "not likely. Be that as it may, I'll help in any case."

"Much thanks to you," Lyvia said cheerfully.

"You'll owe me too for this one," Tate said, pointing at Lyvia.

Lyvia gestured, "anything."

Raj pulled Lyvia away from Tate. "Never tell a Vampire, "anything" when you owe him some help."

"Past the point of no return," Tate said with a smile, "she said it, can't take it back."

"She didn't have a clue," Raj said with a snarl.

"Unwind, Shifter," Tate said with a shake of his head. "I will not have her removed her own head or anything like that... "

"Didn't you have that one person do that?" Dustin asked, watching the Vampire.

Tate chuckled, "that person assaulted and beat a youngster nearly to death. What's more since he owed me an 'anything' favor, I reprimanded him to slash his own head."

The two ladies in the room sucked in a stunned breath.

"He made them come," Tate said with a flick of his wrist.

"I don't believe they're stunned you had a man like that, commit suicide," Dustin said with a snicker. "I believe they're stunned that the man really did it."

The two ladies gestured.

"Well," Tate said with that fiendish smile of his, "I can be exceptionally convincing."

"I trust that," Lyvia said, having been influenced quite a bit by once before when she'd initially met him.

"Hello, this should be a festival!" Raj yelled. "I tracked down my mate," he said then kissed Lyvia. At the point when he lifted his head, he smiled down at her. "Furthermore we're going to the finals!"

The room emitted in cheers, and they returned to celebrating.

~☐~

Lyvia saw her email, her eyes open wide. Sharissa had done it. She'd really pulled it off. She peered down at Symone, who was scouring against her leg.

"How am I going to manage you?" she murmured.

Symone gazed toward her with a clear gaze.

"Much obliged, you're a great deal of help," Lyvia said with a snicker, then, at that point, inclined down and petted her new feline. "I suppose you're eager." She got to her feet and went to the kitchen to get the food she'd purchased for Symone.

"Hello, Mafilia."

Lyvia gazed upward from pouring food to grin at her mate. "Morning, Mafilio."

"If it's not too much trouble, let me know that is not our morning meal," Raj said with a prodding grin as he highlighted the food Lyvia was pouring for the feline.

Lyvia laughed and shook her head. "No. Our morning meal is in the cabinets."

"Allow me to figure, grain chips," he said with a prodding shine in his eyes.

She smiled at him. "You'll need to see with your own eyes."

He went to the cabinets and laughed. "Commander Crunch Berries, decent," he said, then, at that point, pulled the crate down and tracked down two dishes and spoons.

She laughed, "you failed to remember that I really want my sugar as well."

He grunted, "I've met Shifters who don't have sugar in their home. Obviously, they're likewise not so conditioned as you," he said the last part as he turned and winked at her.

She folded her arms over her chest and scowled at him. "I would rather not have any familiarity with your other morning after's."

"Try not to have any," he said, then, at that point, set the dishes and box of cereal on the lounge area table.

"In this way, you're one of the individuals who escape before sunup, huh?" Lyvia asked as she snatched the milk from the ice chest.

At the point when she upheld up, she found something exceptionally hard at her posterior.

"I would rather not talk about my life before you, isn't that right?" he asked as he scoured her hips through her nightshirt.

She gulped, "actually no, not actually."
He pulled her to a standing position then, at that point, turned her toward the table. She set the milk adjacent to the dishes then, at that point, screeched when her shirt went up and her underwear went down.

"I love your butt," he said then smacked it.

Lyvia moaned. She never knew a slap on the ass could be such a turn on.

Raj tumbled to his knees and opened her sweet pussy so he could see it. It was the most astounding pussy he had at any point seen. An astonishing pussy on an astounding feline.

He heard Lyvia murmur and smiled, then, at that point, inclined up and licked her pleasantness, which was at that point trickling down her thighs.

"Blessed fuck," she inhaled out when his tongue contacted her.

He laughed, "you like to say that. Don't you?"

She moaned with delight. "It's something that has in every case just jumped out of my mouth, goodness God, don't stop."

He laughed against her clit, his tongue whirling around it. "You taste and smell like apricots."

"What is it with organic product?" Lyvia asked, then, at that point, shouted out when he maneuvered her clit into his mouth and sucked on it.

Her climax came quick as far as Raj might be concerned would be. She shook and shouted out with delight as she called out to out him. His rooster leaped to consideration, and his Tiger snarled, needing to mount his mate once more.

"Not this time." Raj murmured to his Tiger, then, at that point, stood and pulled his fighters down to free his chicken. She was at that point twisted around the table, actually squirming from her climax. He slapped her butt cheek, which made her screech, and he smiled, then, at that point, gotten her hips and entered her.

"Heavenly fuck!" she shouted out, and he laughed.

He truly loves this lady; he is happy she's his mate. His Tiger is cheerful as well assuming the steady murmuring in his mind said anything.

"Damn, you feel better," he said with a moan as he rammed into her snugness.

He was her first, and that was a greater turn on then any sexual enhancer. To be your mate's first darling is an incredible inclination. He just wished he'd understood it before he'd blasted through her their first time.

"Raj, gracious God, Raj, yes," Lyvia said with an uproarious murmur.

He grinned. Her Tiger was similarly however cheerful as his seemed to be.

"Lyvia," he groaned as he clutched her hips and screwed her over her eating table.

"I can't accept we're fucking in my kitchen," she said with a gasp.

He laughed, "we will screw wherever in this house before we need to leave for my next game."

She laughed, "that sounds like a decent arrangement to me."

"What did you mean with regards to the natural product remark?" he asked when he recollected her prior assertion. He'd been so engaged with eating her he'd neglected to get some information about it.

She chuckled as she turned her head to glance back at him. "Sharissa smells like peaches to Dustin."

He grinned, "I get it's a Fated Mate thing."

She gestured then turned her head forward once more.

"No, I need you to see me like that," he said as he grasped her hair and turned her head to confront him.

Her eyes turned into a smoky dark instead of silvering, and he moaned.

"No doubt about it," he said as he inclined forward and kissed her.

She groaned against his lips. "So are you."

He laughed against her mouth. He wasn't generally enthused about being called lovely, however from his mate, it sounded awesome. Indeed, even his Tiger loved it.

"Harder," she said with a moan.

His Tiger jumped, and Raj needed to utilize each strength he needed to hold him back from dominating and screwed their mate against the table while she's as yet in Human structure.

"Not going to occur, pal," he said with a laugh.

"What's up?" she asked, watching him.

He smiled at her. "My Tiger got somewhat invigorated when you said that."

She grinned, "my Tiger is mauling to come out."

Raj inclined forward so he could murmur in her ear. "In the future, my little Tiger, in the future."

Lyvia's body detonated with sensations when he murmured into her ear. Her Tiger was murmuring so noisy she could scarcely hear whatever else.

"Indeed!" she shouted out when his arms descended on top of hers, his fingers binding with hers as he stuck them to the table and screwed her harder similarly as she'd asked him to. "More." She protested, and he pummeled considerably harder and more profound.

"Sacred fuck!" she shouted as the greatest climax she has at any point had, emitted from her spine.

"Indeed!" he got down on when she fixed around him. He snorted and rammed into her a couple of more occasions, then, at that point, his body shook with his climax, and he spilled his seed somewhere inside her.

Their joined wrists shivered as their solidarity joined and increased.

"That was... " He began to say once he fell against her.

"Unbelievable," she completed for him.

He laughed, "that is single word to utilize."

"Hungry?" she asked, taking a gander at the milk and oat.

"Better believe it, much more now," he said, kissing the side of her neck.

Raj moaned and watched Lyvia fix their dishes of grain while he was as yet hitched inside her. He realizes she's not prepared to begin a family with him, and he gets it. However, the Goddesses expected for them to have enormous families subsequently the tying.

He'd took a stab at slipping a condom on once, which had never been an issue. However, it had skiped off his dick and insulted her. Which he wasn't ready to keep down his giggling, in light of the fact that, come on, who could have?

She'd punched him however at that point handled him to the bed and screwed him from on top. That hitching had been enjoyable. She'd nodded off on top of him while they paused, and he laid down with his mate's bosoms squeezed against his hard chest.

"Shar got a new line of work I can do at home," she said around a significant piece of cereal.

He laughed. He cherished that she wasn't unimposing and against sugar and working out.

"That is great," he said, then, at that point, scooped a huge chomp of cereal into his mouth.

It ought to be abnormal to remain behind his mate with his chicken trapped in her pussy, eating Captain Crunch Berries. Yet, he thought that it is comparably ordinary as expected got for a Shifter with his Fated Mate.

"Work will take up a ton of my time, however I ought to have the option to give you my consideration on breaks... "

"Screw breaks," he said through a mouth loaded with cereal. "I will screw you while you're working, and we'll lay or stand together while we trust that the tying will get done, and you can proceed with your work, then, at that point, we will rehash it."

She laughed.

"I get it's twice as hard for us then it is for Shar and Dustin since she's Human and can indeed take a limited amount a lot. That is to say, since I'm a Shifter and all, the draw is more grounded for me." Lyvia said as she spooned one more chomp of oat into her mouth.

Raj chuckled at that. "Try not to think little of a Human Fated Mate, Mafilia. You fail to remember she has the strength of a Shifter now."

"Right," she said with a gesture. "Be that as it may, does she have the sexual hunger of a female Shifter?"

He set his bowl on the table and inclined forward. "Based on what Dustin's siblings have told me, they have gotten those two in restrooms, the exercise center, their mom's home, the pool, the jacuzzi... "

Lyvia chuckled, "OK, alright. Along these lines, she has everything. Be that as it may, would she be able to do this?" she asked with a devilish smile. She'd felt his bunch mellowing and realized she better do it now, or her Tiger will make some serious trouble for her from morning 'til night.

She moved, and she could hear Raj snarling behind her.

He moved, and her table didn't make due.

Chapter 5

"I can't completely accept that you tracked down your mate," Sebastian Bensing said, scowling at Raj. "You out of most of us."

Raj smiled, "destiny is a bitch."

"No doubt," Daryl protested from the opposite side of the table.

"In any case, she's a shrewd bitch. That is to say, look what she gave us." Dustin said, watching Sharissa and Lyvia.

Raj gestured with a fiendish smile as he inclined toward the bar and requested their beverages.

"Essentially Marry-Beth loves our little Human," Daryl said happily.

"I believe she's desirous," Dominic said with a laugh. "She continues to check out the young ladies then over at both of you with that stink eye of hers.

"She's significantly more seasoned than us, and she hasn't tracked down her mate," Daryl said with a wave to the proprietor of The Shifter Dive.

"Do they have Fated Mates for lesbians?" Drezden pondered without holding back.

The others at the table saw him then, at that point, broke into chuckling.

"You realize I've never thought about that," Dustin said with a shake of his head.

"What are you young men hackling about?" Sharissa asked as she set a plate of beverages on the table.

"Simply contemplating whether the Goddesses made Fated Mates for the equivalent sex as they did us," Dustin said, then, at that point, maneuvered her onto his lap and kissed her.

"Same-sex?" Lyvia asked as she sat in the seat adjacent to Raj.

"No doubt, you know," Dylan said, then, at that point, made the two his clench hands into O's and beat them together.

"Goodness God," Shar said, gazing at Dylan.

He just grinned at her and continued to pound his clench hands together.

"We get it," Lyvia said with a snarl.

Dylan laughed and brought down his hands.

"I didn't realize Marry-Beth was a lesbian," Shar said then turned her head to check out the proprietor of the bar.

"No big surprise she's been taking a gander at us with yearning rather than the folks," Lyvia said with a laugh.

"Indeed, it's the ideal opportunity for me to go," Sebastian said as he checked the time.

"However, you just arrived," Raj said, watching his companion.

Sebastian shrugged, "we're leaving promptly in the first part of the day. I simply needed to meet your lovely mate and tell her she's with some unacceptable person," he said, then, at that point, winked at Lyvia.

Lyvia grinned at him. "In your fantasies, Panther."

Sebastian's hands went to his chest. "Directly through the heart, darlin'."

She laughed, "I was really pointing lower."

"Ugh!" Sebastian snorted as he moved in an opposite direction from the table. "Also at that note, goodnight all. I will be back the following month. All of you better keep your eyes toward the rear of your heads on the grounds that no other person is observing their mate until I get mine."

"You're dreaming in case you believe I'm going to not search for mine while you're gone," Daryl said with a snarl.

Sebastian grunted, then, at that point, checked out Raj and Lyvia. "Well done to both of you. What's more to both of you on the fledgling," he said, grinning at Dustin and Shar.

"Be protected," Shar said from Dustin's lap.

Dustin laid his hand over Shar's level stomach and smiled at Sebastian.

"What's more you," Sebastian said, pointing at Raj, "you have yourself a decent mate there, don't botch it."

Raj smiled and pulled Lyvia against his side. "Try not to plan to."

"Get you all one month from now," Sebastian said, then, at that point, he was no more.

"I must pee," Shar said with a groan, "I think this whelp utilizes my bladder as a trampoline."

Dustin laughed and kissed her cheek. "Will you go with her?" he asked, going to Lyvia.

"Obviously," Lyvia said as she got to her feet.

Shar hopped off Dustin's lap, and the two ladies made a beeline for the restroom, affectionately intertwined.

"They continue to check out our mates like they're a course in a seven-course supper," Raj said with a snarl when he saw pretty much every eye in the bar on their mates.

Dustin gestured, "you must become acclimated to it, sibling. It's the pheromone they put off. Generally your mate, I believe she's in heat."

Raj grunted, "definitely, I think her Tiger is. In any case, Lyvia needs us to get to know one another before we start a family. In any case, with the tying, I don't believe that will occur."

"I realize Shar will very much want to raise our whelp with her companions. For hell's sake, perhaps they'll be mates," Dustin said with a snicker.

"Have you attempted condoms?" Dylan inquired.

Raj grunted and did whatever it takes not to chuckle. "Indeed, and I can't wear condoms with my mate."

"Odd," Daryl said without gazing toward Raj.

"What occurred?" Dustin asked, watching Raj. "I haven't wanted to attempt with Shar."

Raj grunted, "condom flew off the tip of my dick and hit Lyvia in the face."

The table howled uncontrollably.

"Better believe it, I chuckled as well. Until she punched me. However, the sex was wonderful after that," Raj said with a smile.

"How's her Tiger taking to this?" Dominic inquired.

Raj giggled when he thought about her eating table. "We should simply say she's pretty much as enthusiastic as her Human to screw like bunnies."

The men around him chuckled once more.

"I don't think so," Dustin said as he leaped to his feet.

Raj went to where Dustin was looking and snarled somewhere down in his throat. Five Shifters were holding up external the lady's washroom.

"What the hell?!" Raj roared as he leaped to his feet.

"How about we go stop them before the young ladies come out," Dylan said as he got to his feet.

"I vow to the Goddesses, I'm not bringing my mate here any longer," Dustin said as he broke his knuckles.

"Also what have you fine men irritably?" Marry-Beth asked as she approached the six Shifters who looked prepared for a fight.

"Goodness, not a lot, simply a few pricks attempting to focus on our mates," Raj said, highlighting the five men holding up external the ladies' washroom.

Wed Beth took a gander at the five Shifters outside the washroom and feigned exacerbation. "They could be sitting tight for their ladies."

"Truly, you will agree with their stance?" Dustin asked, frowning at the proprietor.

"I'm simply saying," Marry-Beth snapped.

"See, Marry, I know you're desirous that we've tracked down our mates," Dustin said, and the lady scowled at him. "Furthermore I implore that some time or another you track down yours." He said as he lifted his hands noticeable all around. "In any case, Shar's pregnant, and I'm not going to allow those butt sphincters to contact her."

Wed Beth murmured intensely. "Go outdoors," she said with a snarl. "I don't need a solitary table or seat broken." She went to leave, then, at that point, turned around with an authentic grin. "Congratulations on the whelp, Dustin," she said, then, at that point, turned and strolled back to the bar.

"You heard her young men. We go outdoors," Daryl said as he broke his knuckles.

~□~

"There's a lot of folks outside the entryway," Sharissa murmured as she went to take a gander at Lyvia.

Lyvia moved from the dryer over to her companion and looked out the entryway. "Heavenly fuck."

Shar chuckled, and Lyvia feigned exacerbation.

"What do you think they need?" Lyvia inquired.

"Us," Shar murmured.

"Truly? Realizing we have two exceptionally solid mate bond siphoned Shifters?"

Shar snickered, "I like that portrayal of our men."

"How about we stay in here until they're gone. I would rather not fend off handsy men," Lyvia said, then, at that point, strolled over to the two seats set up out of the way.

"Better believe it, I have my offspring to consider now," Shar said as she joined Lyvia.

Lyvia chuckled.

"What?" Shar asked, taking a gander at her companion.

Lyvia shook her head. "Nothing. I just recalled how I'd utilized the reason of you being pregnant, and we didn't realize that you truly were."

Shar laughed. "How long would it be advisable for us to pause?"

"In case they're not gone in five, we'll call the folks."

~ ☐ ~

"Ask them what they're remaining there looking out for," Dustin murmured in Dylan's ear.

Dylan gestured then approached one of the five men outside the washroom.

"Great call," Raj murmured.

Dustin gestured, and they looked as Dylan moved toward the men.

"Hello man," Dylan said as he halted close to the Shifters. "What are you all hanging tight over here for?"

The man nearest to Dylan took a gander at him and giggled. "Haven't you found out about them? There are two unclaimed Fated Mates in the restroom. I've heard that regardless of whether you're not their Fated Mate, the sex is mind blowing."

"Mother lover!" Dustin hollered so clearly, everybody in the bar went to him and his gathering.

"Oooo wrong reply," Dylan said then got back to his sibling's side, "since you see, my sibling here is, indeed, mated to one of those ladies. Furthermore our companion here is mated to the next. Soooo... You're in a bad way."

"Decent discourse," Dominic said with a roll of his eyes.

The five men outside the ladies' washroom snarled.

"Outside!" Marry-Beth yelled at them.

"Why, so they can guarantee the mates? Try not to think so," one of the five men said. "I will screw that fair Human until she drains," he said as he got his groin.

"Apologies, Marry-Beth!" Dustin hollered with a wild snarl. "I'll pay for the damn tables and seats!" Before the man realized what was occurring, Dustin had him noticeable all around and across the bar towards the exit.

"Oh my goodness," Dylan said as he watched the Bear Shifter fly through the air. "I truly need my very own Fated Mate."

The man arrived on a vacant table, say thanks to God.

"You better compensation for that, Dusty!" Marry-Beth screamed.

"Here," Daryl said as he slapped a wad of money on the bar. "For that table and whatever else he might break in transit out the entryway with that poop chute."

Wed Beth moaned, "I heard the thing the ass said about Sharissa. Ensure he pays," she said as she pulled the cash to her.

Daryl gestured, "relax, he will wish he'd never looked at my younger sibling."

Wed Beth gestured, "just, kindly go outdoors."

"Indeed ma'am," Daryl said, then, at that point, gotten back to his different siblings to assist them with accompanying the other four men outside.

"Dustin," Raj said, grabbing hold of his companion's arm.

"Release me, Raj," Dustin snarled.

"Try not to kill him, Dusty," Raj said, fixing his grasp.

"You heard the thing he said about Sharissa. Imagine a scenario where he'd said that regarding Lyvia?" Dustin snarled, scowling at his companion.

Raj gestured. "Indeed, I heard. Furthermore we will kick their butts in general. Yet, you want to recall. In case you kill him, you will go to prison. Also what will Sharissa do alone with your fledgling while the both of you go crazy from not being close to one another?"

Dustin protested. He abhorred it when individuals were correct, particularly when his Cougar looked for from his enclosure.

"Goodness, is a battle a-blending?" everybody diverted as Tate dropped down from the rooftop. "I do adore a decent battle. What are we quarreling over today? Charges?"
"What the hell, Tate?" Dustin asked, gazing at his companion.

Tate grinned, "I was simply minding my beloved mates. Gracious look, that Bear appears as though he needs to remove your head, Dusty. How did you respond?"

"He tossed him across the bar," Dylan said with a laugh.

"Well," Tate said as he turned Dustin upward and down.

Normally, Cougar's aren't generally so solid as Bears, particularly in Human structure. Yet, Dustin should get a lot of lovins from Sharissa.

"What's more for what reason would he do that?" Tate inquired.

"Since he said something regarding Sharissa," Dylan said.

Tate drew nearer to Dustin. An aspect of his responsibilities in this world, it to hold Shifters back from killing each other for dumb reasons.

"What did he say, old buddy?" Tate murmured.

Dustin let Tate know what the butt sphincter had said and what the five men had been doing outside the ladies' washroom. Dustin realizes what Tate's alleged occupation is with regards to Shifters. However, at this moment, he couldn't have cared less in case Tate detached his arms. He can chomp the moronic ass' head off without his arms.

Tate clacked his tongue then, at that point, taken a gander at the Bear Shifter. "Appears as though you have taken on too much all at once, Bear."

"Fuck off, Vampire!"

"Try not to kill him, Dustin. I would rather not go through the late evening attempting to disclose to the seniors why you can't invest energy in jail," Tate said, then, at that point, stepped back.

With a furious snarl, Dustin took off after the Bear. The two men battled, consequences be damned, and perhaps Dustin's life did. Since the Bear had no concerns of investing energy in jail. Be that as it may, Dustin can't be away from

Sharissa for a really long time before the two of them go frantic.

With his additional strength from his mate, Dustin was winning until the other four hopped in.

Chapter 6

"They're gone," Lyvia said as she opened the entryway.

"What was that uproarious accident?" Shar pondered without holding back as they left the washroom.

"Not certain, yet I could swear I'd heard your mate hollering."

Shar gestured, "So did I."

They halted when they saw the confusion of the bar. Tables and seats were fragmented all over by the entry, and individuals were accumulated by the entryway.

"Where are our folks?" Lyvia asked, gazing at their unfilled table.

"I have an inclination that is the thing that everybody is attempting to watch," Shar said, highlighting the gathering at the entryway.

Lyvia checked out the gathering and gestured. "How about we go see what our mates found themselves mixed up with."

Sharissa gestured, and they set out toward the front entryway.

They needed to push through the group, and before they got to the entryway, two men got them.

"Heavenly fuck," Lyvia said when she was pulled against a strong chest.

"Get your hands off me!" Sharissa shouted.

"Release them, you blockheads!"

Lyvia and Shar looked as Marry-Beth hit the one holding Shar over the head with a play club.

"What the heck, Marry-Beth?!" the man shouted out as he let go of Shar.

Lyvia kicked her detainer in the shin, and when he let her go, she imploded against Shar.

"Wouldn't you be able to asses see they're guaranteed?!" Marry-Beth screeched as she highlighted the two ladies' wrists.

The two men checked out the ladies' wrists, and their skin withered.

"Seems as though I really want to set up another sign," Marry-Beth said, watching Shar and Lyvia. "I don't need those young men to quit coming in here, and assuming that their mates are assaulted each opportunity they come here, they will quit coming here. What's more I realize Sebastian will follow," she said with a shake of her head.

"New Bar rule!" Marry-Beth yelled over the clamor of her bar. "Check wrists before you pay attention to your chicken and attempt to guarantee them for yourself! The following individual to assault an asserted mate is getting their dick mounted on the divider so anyone might be able to see!" she dismissed to walk, then, at that point, turned around.

"What's more no cockblocking. Assuming that you attempt to take somebody's mate, more than your dick will be mounted on the divider. In case she's not your mate, remain the damnation away from her!" Marry-Beth yelled.

"Or on the other hand him," Sharissa said when she saw Mable.

Wed Beth followed Sharissa's eyes and snarled. "Or on the other hand him," she said then got back to the bar.

"How about we go," Lyvia said as she grabbed hold of Sharissa's hand.

They pardoned themselves through the remainder of the Shifters, who was attempting to see what was going down outside. Lyvia and Shar made it outside similarly however four Shifters hopped Dustin as he seemed to be severely thrashing another.

"Dustin!" Sharissa shouted and took off towards her mate.

"Hold up there, little mother," Tate said as he delicately folded his arms over Shar.

Dustin heard his mate shout, and his Cougar assumed control over, no if ands or buts. With a boisterous, furious snarl, he moved and flung different Shifters off him.

"Crap," Daryl said, watching his sibling, "in the event that he gets found out, he'll be captured."

"Why?" Shar asked, destroys streaming her cheeks.

"Since despite the fact that Humans endure our quality, they have one guideline," Dylan said.

"Try not to move in broad daylight," every one of the six Shifters said simultaneously.

Shar checked out her siblings. "Help him," she requested.

The siblings giggled, "indeed, ma'am." They said simultaneously, then, at that point, pursued the Shifters, who were all the while attempting to bring Dustin down.

"Try not to kill them!" Tate hollered out to the Kraftman siblings and Raj.

"Which began this?" Shar asked as she watched her mate battle a Shifter who had moved into a Bear.

"The Bear your mate is battling, took steps to screw you until you drained," Tate murmured into her ear.

Lyvia sucked in a stunned breath, then, at that point, gotten a stone and tossed it at the Bear.

The stone hit the Bear in the head and skiped off. The Bear halted its assault on the Cougar and went to them.

"Blessed fuck," Lyvia murmured.

"Great going," Shar protested, "you just irritated a Bear."

The Bear headed towards them, and Lyvia moved. At the point when the Bear got to them, the Tigress was prepared for him.

"Damn it, Lyvia!" Raj hollered as he watched the Bear surge at his mate.

"Tate let us know the thing the poop chute said about me!" Sharissa hollered.

"Extraordinary, fault me," Tate protested.

"Damn it, Vampire," Raj said as he ran towards them. "Did you disregard the mate bond?"

"Not in any manner," Tate said with a smile, "I realized she was kicking the bucket to reach out."

Raj snarled at the Vampire then, at that point, stopped to watch his mate as she hopped on top of the Bear and cut him down. Her teeth sank into the Bear, and the Bear thundered.

"Get off my man!" a lady hollered as she ran out of the bar.

"Your man?" Raj asked, gazing at the lady.

"He'd passed on the table to go to the washroom, and when he didn't return, I went looking and heard he was assaulted by a bunch of Hyenas."

"Hyenas!" Shar shouted. "Cougars!"

The lady took a gander at the Cougar, who was helping his siblings bring down the other four men.

"For what reason are they battling?" the lady inquired. "Furthermore for what reason would she say she is as yet on top of my beau?"

"Miss, I figure you ought to plunk down," Tate said with a giggle.

"Screw you, Vampire. Shouldn't you stop this?"

"I let them know no killing; that is adequate," Tate said with a smile.

"For what reason are you holding that Human?" the lady inquired.

"Interest killed the Bear," Tate said with an underhanded smile.

"Is it accurate to say that they were battling about a damn Human?!"

"Heads up," Raj said, strolling towards her, "that Human turns out to be my companion's Fated Mate."
Her eyes ran from Raj over to Shar and back once more. "Anyway, they are battling about her?"

"Not battling about her," Tate said, his hold fixing around Shar when she moved to help Lyvia. The Bear shook the Tiger away from him, and Lyvia arrived on her in those days turned over and remained with a snarl.

Raj let the lady know what her "beau" had said about Shar, and the lady snarled uproariously.

"Is it true that you are certain she's mated to the Cougar?"

Tate held Shar's arms up so the lady could see the markings.

"Assuming you all had been a long time prior, you'd have heard Dustin's declaration." Raj said as he strolled towards his mate and remained among her and the bear.

"Allow me to deal with this," the lady said, then, at that point, moved into her bear and assaulted her beau.

Which they were almost certain would have been unloaded like a sack of rocks.

Alarms rang in the evening, and Raj took a gander at Lyvia. "Shift back," he said.

Lyvia moved back to her Human structure, and Raj pulled her against him.

"That was exceptionally moronic," he said, holding her.

She chuckled, "I know, yet it was enjoyable."

Raj grunted, "it was additionally attractive as hellfire."

"Well," Lyvia said with a murmur.

The two Bears kept on battling before them. The female nailed the male down and spot his ear. The male shouted, and she let him go, then, at that point, moved back to her Human structure.

"Leave that alone an update!" she thundered at him. "Nobody undermines me! Nobody!" she shouted, then, at that point, raged away towards the parking area.

"Dustin requirements to move back!" Daryl hollered.

"Release me," Shar said when she saw her mate walking forward and backward on the walkway.

Tate let her go, and she rushed to Dustin.

"Dustin," she murmured as she set her hand on his shoulder.

Dustin snarled when she contacted him then, at that point, whimpered when she hopped back from him. The Cougar moved towards his mate and scoured his head against her chest.

Shar grinned, "you're so lovely. However, you truly need to move before the cops arrive," she said as she scoured the highest point of his head.

The Cougar sat on his rear legs and began to move.

"Dustin," Shar cried as she fell into her mate's arms.

"Sharissa," he inhaled, holding her nearby.

The alarms had halted, and two vehicles pulled facing the check.

"Time for me," Tate said as he strolled over to the four officials who got out of the vehicles.

"How is he going to deal with them?" Shar asked as she watched.

"Cause them to fail to remember what they saw. Cause them to accept it was only a standard bar brawl, and it had separated before they got here," Dustin said as he cuddled her neck.

"How are we going to get that ass to move back?" Raj asked as he and Lyvia joined Dustin and Shar.

"Don't have a clue and couldn't care less," Dustin protested.

"I need to see your wrists!" a Shifter who had been battling them snarled as he approached the two couples.

Lyvia, Raj, Dustin, and Shar held out their wrists simultaneously. Their palms up so the butt sphincters could see their mate's names and let them the hellfire be.

The man's face withered, and he stepped back. "I believe it's the ideal opportunity for me to return home," he said, then, at that point, took off at a run.

Lyvia and Shar laughed as they watched the Shifter run down the road.

"I can't completely accept that this bologna we go through. Perhaps we should remain at home from now into the foreseeable future," Sharissa said with a frown.

"No chance," Raj said with a devilish smile. "I'm not stowing away, nor is my mate," he said, pulling Lyvia closer.

"The other three took off when that one did," Dylan said with a snicker as he went along with them.

Tate strolled over to them, and they looked as the squad cars drove away.

"He actually hasn't moved?" Tate asked as his head gestured towards the Bear, who sat alone out of the way.

"No," Raj said as he folded his arms over Lyvia and set his jaw on the highest point of her head.

"I'll deal with it," Tate said, then, at that point, strolled over to the Bear and looked at him without flinching and began conversing with him.

"How would we know we're not generally under that man's spell?" Raj asked, watching the Vampire.

"Since we'd be generally some type of strolling Zombies," Dustin said with a snicker.

Raj grunted, "I presume."

The Bear moved into his Human structure, then, at that point, turned without a word and left them.

"What did you tell him?" Lyvia asked when the Vampire rejoined them.

"To move back and forget all that he'd seen and done this evening. To avoid any Fated Mate he smells. Except if it's his own. Also return home and not at any point return to this bar," Tate said with a shrug.

"Will he tune in?" Shar inquired.

"He better in the event that he knows what's useful for him," Dustin said, then, at that point, taken in his mate's fragrance.

"That is upsetting," Dylan said as he grimaced at his sibling.

Dustin laughed, "simply delay until you track down your mate."

"Consider what might have occurred on the off chance that Tate hadn't been here," Raj said as he glanced around at his companions.

"Dustin would have killed the Bear Shar would have gotten herself injured attempting to help him, and we'd be in every way in prison at this moment," Daryl said with a shake of his head.

"OK, this evening is going in my 'never happening again' document," Shar said as a chill ran down her spine.

"Darling," Dustin said as he kissed her cheek, "you're mated to a Shifter. Trust me, this will happen once more."

~□~

"Remember to change Symone's gauze two times every day," Lyvia said as her mate attempted to drag her out the entryway.

"She knows all of this, Lyvia. You've been rehashing it for the beyond two days," Raj said as he at last got his mate to the entryway.

"Gracious, and on the off chance that the gathering is awful, the number to the inn is..."

"On the cooler. Indeed, I know," Shar said cheerfully. "Take great consideration of her, Raj."

Raj showed respect to her, "with my life."

"So sweet," Lyvia said, gazing toward her mate.

"Indeed, I am, presently how about we go."

"Symone, you pay attention to Sharissa and Dustin! I'll miss all of you!"

"They know, come on," Raj said as he hauled her to the vehicle.

Shar and Dustin waved to their companions as they pulled out of the drive.

"Is it accurate to say that you are certain you're good with us watching Symone and her cats until they get back?"

Dustin grinned down at her. "She's catlike, so obviously I am. Presently, assuming it had been a canine... "

She snickered, "I don't see a Tiger coexisting with a canine."

He laughed, "right, you are."

Chapter 7

"Do you figure Symone will be OK?" Lyvia asked as she turned in her seat and watched Dustin's carport vanish.

Raj grunted. "You messing with me? You just left her with a Cougar and his mate, who's anticipating a fledgling. Those felines will be excessively coddled."

Lyvia snickered. "You're correct," she said as she turned and sat in her seat.

"Are you going to be alright?" he asked, intertwining her hand with his.

She gestured. "That's right. I'm with you," she said with a splendid grin.

"Smart response," he said, then, at that point, crushed her hand.

"Is it accurate to say that you are certain you will not cause problems for bringing me along?"

"That is why we have Tate," he said cheerfully.

"Gracious no doubt, the IOU, I guaranteed."

He gestured, "ideally, he will not request anything amazing."

She shuddered, "he's a Vampire. I have an inclination anything he does is abnormal."

Raj laughed, "indeed, yet he's faithful to his companions. So perhaps he'll back off of you."

She grinned. "I never suspected I'd be companions with a Vampire or track down my mate," she said as she radiated at him.

He smiled back.

At the point when they got to the air terminal, Raj left his vehicle in the parcel with the remainder of his group's vehicles, then, at that point, they ran inside and scarcely got to their plane before they shut the entryways.

"Next time I'm pressing you in a bag while you're snoozing," Raj said when they got to their seats.

She laughed and plunked somewhere near the window.

"No time like the present you arrived," Alec said as he strolled down the path towards them.

"Alec," Raj said happily, "I'd like you to meet my mate Lyvia. Lyvia, this is the main other Shifter in the group, Alec."

"Ideal to meet you," Lyvia said happily as she held her hand out to the Shifter.

"Damn, this will be inconvenience," Alec said, shaking her hand.

"What?" Raj inquired.

"Check out you," Alec murmured, "the plane has Shifters all over the place, and you brought your mate locally available. What's more she's in heat."

Raj checked out them and snorted. "Poo."

"I'm not in heat," Lyvia murmured.

Alec inclined in towards her and sniffed the air around her. "Trust me, honey, you're not kidding."

Lyvia grimaced.

"You ought to have left her at home," Alec said as he stood up.

"Can't." Raj said once he was sufficiently close to his companion. "We'd both go crazy," he said as he held his wrists up for Alec to check out them. "You've perused similar books I have."

Alec whistled as he took a gander at the markings on Raj's wrists. "OK, so everything is valid?"

Raj gestured cheerfully. "Gracious no doubt."

"Indeed, I surmise I'll take this unfilled seat behind you. For good measure."

Raj gestured, "much obliged, mate."

"Are we at serious risk?" Lyvia asked when Raj plunked down next to her.

He grinned at her, "simply remain nearby me."

She gestured, then, at that point, inclined toward him and shut her eyes.

"Knock her up, then, at that point, you will not need to stress," Alec murmured into Raj's ear once they were noticeable all around.

Raj gestured. There is nothing he wouldn't need more than to do precisely that. In any case, he should regard his mate's desires. Not that he has a lot to say about it in any case, he can't wear a condom. Furthermore he realizes she'd began the pill a couple of days prior he'd thought that it is in her best in class. In this way, it's completely out of his hands until further notice.

~□~

"Go, Raj!" Lyvia yelled as she hopped up from her seat to root for her mate.

The game was going excitingly well, they were ahead three to one, and it was the last quarter. Raj and his companion Alec made an objective, and Lyvia bounced all over whistling and cheering.

Fortunately, they hadn't had any difficulty from different Shifters on the plane ride here. Additionally, fortunately, that will be the main plane ride until they head home in light of the fact that even in rest, she'd been anxious as hellfire that somebody planned to kill Raj and his companion to get to her.

She realizes Raj had seen the conception prevention pills in her first rate, the garments around them had been rumpled. She hasn't taken one yet; she doesn't know whether she would rather not start a family with her mate. Of course, they don't have the foggiest idea about one another that well yet, however he's her mate. What other man would she say she will have a family with?

She watched the commencement for the finish of the game briefly, then, at that point, her eyes focused in on her mate. He went to her and made a gesture of blowing her a kiss then, at that point, made the last objective of the game similarly as the ringer went off. They won five to one.

The group ejected with serenades, and Lyvia smiled as she paid attention to the group, serenade her mate's name over and over.

"Did you see him blow that kiss at me?" a lady said from behind Lyvia.
"No, he was pantomiming blowing a kiss at me," one more said.

Lyvia went to the voices and found six puck rabbits who were battling about who Raj had blown the kiss to.

Lyvia smiled, "really, women, he was blowing it to me."

"Dream on," a rabbit said with a grunt.

"Hello, would you say you aren't the skank who continued to squeeze her body against the glass the week before? Definitely, similar to that will prevail upon Raj," the rabbit said with a growl.

Lyvia laughed then snarled at them. Each of the six ladies got away from her. She grinned, then, at that point, headed towards the exit of the ice arena to get together with her mate.

She could hear the rabbits not far behind her and feigned exacerbation.

"Raj, Raj!" the rabbits called out as they pushed past Lyvia.

"That kiss was for me, wasn't it?" one of the sluttier rabbits murmured as she grabbed hold of Raj's arm and inclined toward him.

In any case, Raj exclusively desired Lyvia. "As a matter of fact, no," he said as he pulled his arm liberated from the rabbit. "It was for my better half," he said as he moved towards Lyvia. "Things being what they are, how was I?"

Lyvia smiled then kissed him. "Great," she murmured against his lips.

"How did that skank's awful showcase last week win her a Hockey player that no other rabbit has packed away?" one of the rabbits murmured, not understanding that the two Shifters could hear her.

Lyvia snarled and followed them. Raj grabbed hold of her arm and went to the rabbits.

"I would see the value in it assuming you didn't consider my better half a skank or a rabbit. She's not one or the other. There is an association with Shifters and their Fated Mates that no Human except for a mate oneself will at any point comprehend." Raj sniffed the air and shook his head.

"Which not a solitary one of you are. So ease the fuck off and quit talking crap about my mate or I'll have you eliminated from each game, and trust me, I have my methodologies." Raj wrapped up with a snarl.

Every one of the six rabbits withered as they took a gander at the two of them, and the glinting silver of their eyes had each of the six rabbits going crazy.

"Good gracious, they're Shifters," a rabbit said, then, at that point, the six females left looking for another player.

Lyvia laughed, "decent taking care of there, Romeo."

He giggled, "come on, we must meet everybody at the transport in fifteen."

"Where do I pause while you're evolving?"

"There's a parlor in the storage space. You can stand by there."

She gestured, "OK."

"I host to go to the after-get-together," he said as he showed her to the room. "In any case, from that point forward, I'm all yours," he said with a fiendish smile.

She grinned back. "The inn will get grievances this evening on the grounds that your playing has me all worked up," she said as she inclined toward him.

Raj snarled, then, at that point, kissed her rapidly on the lips and strolled to his storage to change.

Lyvia laughed. He's in for a universe of marvel this evening, and she's not halting at one time. Perhaps she will begin a family with her mate. What's more they'll begin on it: this evening.

~□~

The get-together passed by excessively delayed for Lyvia. She was unable to hold back to get her hands on Raj and tear his garments from his provocative as wrongdoing body. When the party faded away, she for all intents and purposes hauled him by his ear to their room.

"That is no joke," Raj said with a snicker when they went into their room.

"I need to begin a family," she exclaimed as she sniffed up his neck, "this evening."

He stopped. "Are you certain?" he asked as his hands gradually moved to hold her arms so she would remain still.

Be that as it may, she wouldn't have any of it. She grabbed hold of him and turned him so quick he lost his equilibrium, then, at that point, she threw Raj onto the bed and jumped on him.

"I let you know the lodging would get grumblings this evening," she said as she sniffed from his navel to his ear.

He snorted. "What might be said about the pills?"

She stopped and checked out him. "I realized you'd tracked down them."

He snorted.

"In any case, yet you didn't say anything," she said, then, at that point, licked his jaw, and his Tiger snarled.

"I let you know it was dependent upon you," he said as he grasped her hips to stop her shaking against his hard cockerel so he could converse with her. He investigated her eyes. "Is it true that you are certain with regards to this?"

She gestured, and Raj's heart took off. He'd been so tragic when he'd tracked down the pills. He dreaded she'd never be prepared to begin a family with him.

"I haven't taken one," she murmured into his ear, and his body trembled.

"You haven't?" he inquired.

She shook her head, her hair zooming around her face.

He grinned as he came to up and tucked the ringlets behind her ears so he could see her eyes.

"Why not?" he murmured.

She shrugged, "in light of the fact that I didn't know whether what I was believing was genuine or simply nerves. That is to say, I didn't think I'd at any point track down anybody to go through my time on earth with, not to mention my mate."

He gestured. He felt the same way. "Thus, we will go after our own fledgling this evening, huh?" he asked with a brassy smile.

She chuckled. "No doubt, that was the arrangement. Presently shut up and screw me," she said, then, at that point, handled him.

They snarled and mewed and murmured and moved around as garments flew all around the room.
She didn't know whether her undies were pulled off or ripped off. Regardless, they were bare, and afterward he was inside her and considerations of everything except her mate, and this second left her brain.

He did as she told him and screwed her great and hard. He was so somewhere inside her that in case they didn't make a whelp this evening, something wasn't right with her.

"Damn, Lyvia, you feel mind boggling."

She mewed as her back angled to his developments. He hammered profound and hard inside her, and she shouted out his name when her climax assumed control over her body and brain.

At the point when she descended from the climax, he was holding her nearby and moving inside her as though he'd kick the bucket assuming he didn't screw her until the two of them fell from weariness.

"Lyvia!" he shouted out as his body shook with his climax. "Fuck, yes!"

"Sacred Fuck!" she shouted out when one more climax emitted from her body.

He laughed at her words as he returned to earth, his rooster actually siphoning his seed somewhere inside her. He pushed his hips forward a couple of times before his bunch shut down all development.

"That was exceptional," she said winded.

He snorted, "better believe it."

She folded her arms and legs over him. "Do you think we made sufficient clamor?"

He giggled as he kissed her nose. "I suspect as much."

She gestured, "great, we'll rehash it shortly."

He grinned down at her. "In case we keep this up, they'll show us out of here bare."

She smiled up at him. "Then, at that point, we'll fuck on their front yard."

He chuckled so hard his side hurt. What had he done to merit this lady? God, he adores her. He stopped. Damn, he truly adores her. Go figure he's overwhelmed with passion, in affection with his mate.

~□~

The following morning, they didn't have any grumblings about them at the front work area, however they got many gazes, and a portion of the ladies in the entryway licked their lips at Raj.

Lyvia smiled as she clung to his side and frowned at the ladies. "Apologies, women, he's taken," she said with a grin.

The ladies muttered about him being a nonconformist, and she turned on them with a snarl.

"He might be a nonconformist as you say, however he's my nonconformist. In this way, you bitches, ease the fuck off!"

The ladies' eyes developed wide when Lyvia snarled regionally.

"Lyvia," Raj said with a laugh, then, at that point, grabbed hold of her arm. He took a gander at different ladies and saw the silver eyes and knew why she was by and large so regional and smiled.

Her Tiger was going to bat for her mate to different Shifters. Which just made him love her considerably more. Since wasn't that what he and Dustin were doing only a couple of days prior?

He checked out the other female Shifters and grinned. "Apologies, women, however I've been guaranteed," he said as he held his and Lyvia's arms up.

The Shifter females sucked in stunned breaths when they saw the fortified markings. A portion of the ladies' heads calculated down, and others looked out of the way. Two kept on gazing at the markings.

"May I see?" one of the females inquired.

Raj saw his mate than at the lady. "We have a transport to get, however certain you can have a brief glance."

Lyvia growled, however the lady didn't go for Raj; she grabbed hold of Lyvia's hands and turned them palms up. She then, at that point, taken a gander at the word UNITY on her right wrist, then, at that point, checked out her left wrist and read her mate's name, RAJ.

"You know why the name is on the left wrist, don't you?" the lady asked, grinning at Lyvia.

Lyvia shook her head, astounded at how decent the lady was being, and seen that her silver eyes didn't look right to be a Shifter.

"Since like the Human's wedding ring is to their left side ring finger, this is straightforwardly associated with your heart," the lady said happily.

Lyvia grinned, "that seems OK."

"In the event that adoration isn't shared, you will go crazy," she cautioned them.

"Try not to need to stress over that," Raj said, pulling Lyvia to his side.

The lady grinned, "indeed, I see that. It's in your eyes," she said, then, at that point, taken a gander at Lyvia. "However, you, my dear, you are as yet befuddled. You need to begin that family with your mate, yet the thing you're perusing as something to satisfy your mate, you're denying yourself that affection."

Lyvia become flushed, and Raj gazed at her. Did she not love him?

"Try not to take my statement adversely, Raj Cunningham. She knows her own sentiments. She simply needs to comprehend them better. However, both of you better catch that transport," she said cheerfully.

"You're not a Shifter," Lyvia murmured.

The lady checked out them then, at that point, grinned at Lyvia. "Exceptionally keen."

"Witch," Raj said, then, at that point, made a stride back and pulled Lyvia with him.

The lady grinned and drew nearer to them once more. "A White Witch. You don't have anything to fear from me. I actually prefer to tuck away among the Shifters. See what I can see."

"What do you see with us?" Lyvia asked as she pulled away from Raj and drew nearer to the Witch.

The Witch grinned, "you are pursuing for that family, yet it will not occur when you need it to. It will come to you when you are prepared and no sooner. You are at this point not in heat, so Shifters ought to withdraw now."

"Much obliged to you," Lyvia said, one eyebrow raised, "I think."

The lady laughed, "be protected, Lyvia. Furthermore recall that you don't need to fear your sentiments."

Lyvia gestured and held her hand out to the lady. "Will I at any point see you once more?"

The Witch grinned and shook Lyvia's hand. "I speculate you will. I see myself searching for something, and it will carry me to you once more. In any case, you should go now, your mentor is hanging tight for you."

"Damn it!" Raj snarled, then, at that point, grabbed hold of Lyvia's arm and hauled her from the lodging.

"Pause, what's your name?" Lyvia called out.

Pearl. I am Pearl Owens. I will see you once more, Lyvia Yule.

Lyvia flickered. She's known about Witches attacking personalities like a Vampire with the exception of Vampires can just infiltrate a Human's psyche. As he does with Shar. Besides with Shar having Dustin's capacities and strength of body and brain, he can just enigmatically guess what she might be thinking.

He can't place considerations into her head or totally assume responsibility for her.

Chapter 8

"Did she do something to you?" Raj asked, watching her face. Assuming that Witch hurt his mate, he's going to...

"No, no," Lyvia said with a chuckle, "she just sent me her name through my brain."

He moaned with alleviation. However pleasant as the lady seemed to be, he didn't confide in Witches. Regardless of whether she say, she's a White Witch.

"Where the fuck have you been, Cunningham!?" the Coach yelled when Raj and Lyvia got to the transport.

"Apologies, Coach. Experienced difficulty looking at," Raj said as he and his mate ventured onto the transport.

"I'm certain it had something to do with all the commotion both of you were making the previous evening!" one of Raj's colleagues yelled from the rear of the transport, making everybody hoot and holler.

Raj saw Lyvia's cheeks turn a dazzling red and snarled. "Can it, or I'll return there and make you suck your own dick."

"Oooooooo," everybody said as they checked out the speaker toward the back.

"It's alright, Raj," Lyvia said as she grasped his hand and grinned at the others. "They're simply desirous on the grounds that you don't need to pay for sex. Furthermore you can have it at whatever point and any place you need," she said with a murmur. She grinned at him, then, at that point, thudded herself down in an unfilled seat and pulled him down next to her. She inclined towards him as she pulled him to her and kissed him.

Yells and whistles emitted, and the Coach yelled for quietness. "Kindly avoid fucking your sweetheart on the transport, Cunningham!"

Raj laughed as he pulled back from Lyvia's kiss and kissed her on the button. "God, I love you."

She took a full breath and laid her head on his shoulder. Raj moaned and kissed the highest point of her head. The Witch had said to have tolerance with her.

"I love you as well," she murmured then shut her eyes.

Raj smiled. Indeed! He thought, then, at that point, shut his eyes and laid his cheek against her head.

~□~

The following not many weeks passed by quick. Raj was kicking ass on the ice, and they were fucking similar to hares in the lodgings. Yet at the same time, Lyvia wasn't pregnant. She dreaded she could never give her mate any fledglings, and it put her into a downturn.

She realizes Raj could feel her downturn, and when they had intercourse, he ensured she was pleasured to the place of practically dropping. However, it didn't stop her contemplations of how she's not an adequate mate. She can't give him an offspring.

"Lyvia," Raj murmured to her one evening. Three weeks after they'd began pursuing for a family.

"What," she sneezed.

He pulled her nearer. "Recall what Pearl had said? It will happen when we're prepared."

"Yet, I am prepared, Raj. More than prepared to have your fledgling," she said with a sniff.

He moaned vigorously, "I know, Mafilia, I know."

"Possibly I'm defaulted, and you should exchange me for a more up to date model. I'm 88 years of age, all things considered."

He shook his head. "What of it. My mother was more than 100 when she had me. Furthermore I'm 98."

She laughed, "we're a few old farts attempting to begin a family."

He grunted, "watch who you call an old fart."

She snickered when he began to stimulate her.

"Other than," he said as he tenderly kissed her, "Dustin is 96."

She murmured, "with a 24 year-old Human."

Raj snarled as he moved her onto her back and stuck her to the bed. "Enough of this pity party Lyvia Yule. A WITCH let you know that you will have my offspring, we simply need time."

She scowled, "it's been three weeks."

"Lyvia, you realize I love you, yet you're being nuts. We have two additional matches to dominate, then, at that point, the title. I would rather not stress over my mate while I'm playing."

Lyvia gestured; she has been so self centered. Not exclusively was he managing their absence of a family, however he additionally has Hockey to ponder. From now into the foreseeable future, her brain will be on the game.

Then, at that point, she'll sulk around about not giving her mate a whelp.

"Alright, Mafilio, no really sulking, and crying. We focus on your games and keep on amazingly like bunnies. Who knows, perhaps it will occur."

He smiled, "there's my mate. Come here."

She smiled with joy and considered nothing for the following hour except for her mate and what he does to her body.

~□~

"Go, Raj!" Lyvia got down on about fourteen days after the fact at the title game.

She's so pleased with him. What's more his group also, obviously. They're astounding on the ice. She can hardly wait until they have little ones rooting for their daddy as he skates around the arena like a master ice skater shooting the puck into the net over and over. Goodness God, and remember the ramming of players against the glass. Damn, that turns her on.

An odd inclination moved through her body, and she multiplied over. What the heck?

~□~

A recognizable smell filled the field, and Raj gazed toward the stands at his mate. She was twisted around, her face making painfilled looks.

"Damn it!" he reviled.

"Head in the game, Cunningham!"

Raj could scarcely inhale, and his Tiger needed out; he nccdcd his mate. Presently!

"She's in heat once more," Alec said as he skated over to Raj.

Raj gestured. "The initial time was the point at which we'd associated, so she hadn't felt its aggravation, simply the appetite of needing me," Raj said as he gazed toward his mate once more, who was in a ton of torment. "Just our mating can stop her aggravation," he said with a snarl.

Alec gestured, "yet you can't screw her here."

Raj scoffed, "I can't let the group down, all things considered."

"Alec, Raj, get your butts off the ice, presently!" their mentor cried.

Raj and Alec skated over to their mentor.

"I really want a telephone," Raj said as he moved over the low divider.

"You needn't bother with a telephone!" the mentor hollered. "What you really want is to get your head on the title!"

"Sir, with all due regard, on the off chance that I don't utilize a telephone and soon, I will stroll off this ice, title or no title," Raj said with a snarl.

"Raj," Alec said, tapping his companion's arm.

"I mean it, Alec. Lyvia is more significant...
"

"I know, look," Alec said, highlighting where Lyvia remained in the stands.

"Mother lovers!" Raj thundered when he saw a few guys moving toward his mate. In her perspective, she'll struggle warding them off. "Give me your telephone!" Raj shouted as he held his hand out to his mentor.

The man was gazing up at the stands where Lyvia was. "You can't go off the deep end on me in light of the fact that your better half is a prostitute," the Coach said.
Raj balled his clench hand to hit the man, yet Alec pulled him back.

"Hitting the Coach will not take care of your concern," Alec murmured in his ear.

"No, however it will cause me to feel soo great," Raj snarled.

"You really want to get your head in the damn game!" the Coach said, looking from Raj to Lyvia and back once more.

Raj went to his mate and snarled a wild snarl that was heard in the stands. The men encompassing her stopped when they heard it.

"Mentor," Alec said with an unnatural quiet; since he realized his companion wouldn't have the option to talk pleasantly to their mentor right now. Not with his mate in peril in the stands. Raj moved to move over the glass divider, and Alec halted him. "We are not Human as you surely understand," Alec said as he pulled his companion away from the glass.

A cheer emitted on the opposite side, and the Coach reviled. "They're winning since both of you can't get your heads out of pussy..."

"My mate is in heat, and each poop chute Shifter here will attempt to assault her!" Raj shouted in his Coach's face.

The man's face withered as he ventured into his pocket for his telephone. "Alright, for what reason didn't you say as much? You realize I set out to find out about Shifters when both of you joined the group."

Raj took the telephone from his Coach and dialed the one individual he knew could help.

"Who the fuck is this, and how could you get my number?!"

Raj smiled, "I want your assistance. Presently!" he hollered the final word into the telephone.

The Vampire showed up before him, and everybody in the space heaved.

"This should be significant," Tate protested as he hung up his telephone.

"Sniff the air and gaze upward there," Raj said as he pointed towards his mate, where the Shifter guys were attempting to contact her. She was warding them off however scarcely. Some left when she showed them her wrists, and others were excessively imbecilic.

Tate took in a full breath and turned towards the stands. "You'll owe me once more," he said, then, at that point, vanished.

Raj moaned with help when Tate showed up alongside Lyvia.

Lyvia bounced when she felt a hand on her shoulder. She turned and heaved when she saw the Vampire.

"Tate," she shouted out then bounced into his defensive arms.

"It's OK, little Tiger," Tate said cheerfully as he held her, then, at that point, gazed toward the four men who were licking their lips as though she was a full feast. He so abhors letches.

"You don't need any of this, young men," Tate said as he investigated every one of their eyes. "This youngster is ensured by me and her mate. Except if you need to bite the dust, I'd encourage you to leave."

"What's more the thing would you say you will do about it, Vampire?"

"I will suck all of you dry assuming you don't ease the fuck off," Tate said as he inclined in to investigate every one of their silver eyes. "You truly don't need that, presently isn't that right?"

"No, we don't need that," the four men said simultaneously, then, at that point, turned and left to get back to their seats.

"Try not to believe that will be the remainder of them."

"What's going on?" Lyvia asked as her stomach fixed once more.

"You're in heat, Lyvia, my dear," Tate said, holding her nearby.

"However, yet it didn't feel this terrible the initial time," she said with a groan.

"Since you had quite recently tracked down your mate and was in a screw free for all of sorts," Tate said with a laugh.

"For what reason does it need to hurt so a lot?" she asked with a wheeze.

"Since it's your body planning for the existence you should make. I would figure you would have the Ice Star's whelp at this point."

Lyvia cried, "we've been attempting."

Tate moaned, "it is the Goddesses. They have their hands on this one."

She gazed toward him with an odd look, and he chuckled then kissed her temple.

"Later, little Tiger, later. At this moment, what about we get you associated with your mate, so the torment dies down."

Her face lit up. "You can do that?"

He laughed then drove her down to the glass. Raj showed up and beat on the glass with his glove.

"Lyvia!" Raj hollered.

"Raj!" she shouted out as she raced to the glass and squeezed her body against it.

"I will dominate this match for you, then, at that point, we're going directly to the lodging," he said as he watched her mound and for all intents and purposes assault the opposite side of the glass.

"Please," she asked, then, at that point, licked the glass.

"Before long, child, soon," he guaranteed, then, at that point, returned to the game.

Having Tate with his mate, he could focus on the game. Tate had been the principal heavenly animal he could imagine to help him. He had the option to get to them quick, and his mate's pheromones won't influence him.

"Raj!" Alec hollered as he passed the puck.

Raj brought his musings completely to the game and still up in the air than any time in recent memory to dominate this match.

"He looks so provocative when he's on the ice," Lyvia said, then, at that point, licked the glass once more.

Tate laughed. A chemical administered Shifter is interesting to watch. Really awful there's not a greater amount of them. Indeed, Shifters without mates go into heat. In any case, in no way like a Fated Mate. Besides, he has an inclination there's another side to this little Tiger then they know.

"Raj!" Lyvia shouted as she beat on the glass. "Kick their butts so we can fuck!"

Tate chuckled when he saw the expression all over, then, at that point, his cheeks turned a dazzling red.

"Excuse me, ma'am. You can't be here... "

"It's okay," Tate said as he strolled over to the Human safety officer and investigated his eyes. "Return to your post; this young woman has authorization to be here."

The man gestured. "Authorization to be here," he said, then, at that point, dismissed and strolled.

"Me and Shar should utilize you on our chief," Lyvia said as she watched Tate.

"Really?" Tate asked, fascinated.

Lyvia gestured, "somebody has been screwing with our reports, and the manager thinks we should simply fix it, however when we do, they mess it up once more. He will not investigate it."

"Gee," Tate said cheerfully, "seems like a secret to me. I'll consider it."

Her eyes extended. "Truly?"

"Sure," he said with a smile, "I do cherish gathering IOUs."

She grunted, "ought to have realized it wasn't out of kinship."

Tate's heart throbbed at that. Alright, he hadn't understood the young ladies considered him a companion. How fascinating. "Perhaps I'll help it as out to you and Shar. A present for the mama to be."

She grinned at him, and his heart expanded. Alright, these Shifters and Human mates are getting to him. Yet, sufficiently astounding, he's not irritated by it.

Lyvia shouted, which took him back to what in particular was continuing. He glanced around and tracked down no aggressors. Lyvia was beating on the glass, supporting her mate. He gazed toward the scoreboard and saw that inside the most recent thirty seconds of the game, Raj had slid the puck into the net, making the triumphant shot.

"Raj!" Lyvia shouted as loud as possible, making Tate cover his ears.

Raj lost his stuff in the ice once his partners had put him down and skated over to the glass, where Lyvia was squeezing herself against it once more.

"Much appreciated, Tate," Raj said, grinning at the Vampire.

Tate shrugged, "simply recollect you owe me for sure."

Raj gestured then turned his eyes to his mate. "You prepared, darling?"

Lyvia licked the glass, and Tate laughed. "That is horny Tiger represent... 'Indeed, child, take me now.'"

Chapter 9

"Cautious Mafilia," Raj said with a laugh as they went into their lodging, and Lyvia bounced on his back.

"Screw me," she snarled.

He laughed, "I will when I step out of my pullover. I didn't have the opportunity to shower... "

"No shower!" she shrieked, then, at that point, licked his ear cartilage.

Raj protested as he set out toward the bed. He'd requested that his partners assemble his poo for him while he took his wild sex-driven mate back to the lodging. Indeed, obviously, he's sex driven too yet not however much he'd been the point at which they'd originally seen as one another.

"Screw me, Raj," she whimpered.

"I'm going to, child, trust me, I am, however I smell... "

"You couldn't have cared less about smelling the first... "

He cut her off by throwing her onto the bed. "As a matter of fact, I did. For what reason do you think I was bare when you tracked down me? I'd raced into the shower before our companions got you to the storage space."

"Gracious," she said with a murmur, "yet I like it when you're all damp with sweat subsequent to dominating a match."

He peered toward her. "You do?"

She gestured as she got to her knees and begun yanking on his pullover. "Extremely attractive," she said, then, at that point, licked his sweat-soaked stomach.

"Fuck, Lyvia."

"Indeed, if it's not too much trouble, screw Lyvia," she murmured.

He laughed, "you're insane when you're toward the start of your hotness. You realize that?"

She gestured, "screw me."

He snarled, "in case you continue to say that, I will not have the option to do any foreplay to get all of you wet... "

"Screw me!" she shouted as loud as possible.

"Screw this," he snarled, then, at that point, thrown his pullover to the floor and strippcd out of his garments. At the point when he remained before her bare, she snatched his pounding rooster and pulled him toward her.

"Presently your turn," he said as he went for her garments.

She shook her head as she got his hips and pulled him down on top of her. He moaned when his cockerel nearly slid immediately inside her.

"Lyvia... " All idea left his brain when she pushed down and pierced herself with his chicken.

"Sacred fuck!" she shouted out.

He laughed. He cherished everything about Lyvia, even her peculiar jests.

"Lyvia," Raj snarled, his Tiger over-eager to mate with their mate. He'd been the hardest to battle through this entire thing.

"Screw me," she snarled as she continued on his chicken.

"Whatever my mate needs," he said, then, at that point, snatched her hips and moved quick and hard.

"Indeed!" she shouted out.

"Good lord, you're more tight than common this evening," he said as he got a move on.

"I'm in heat," she murmured as though it was confidential.

He laughed. He adored his mate when she was in heat. Nearly however much he adored her some other day.

"Raj!" she cried as she moved with him. "I'm going to cum!"

"Indeed, kindly do," he snorted as he pressed her hips and moved harder and more profound.

How he'd so effortlessly wound up inside her with her garments still on was past him. She more likely than not avoided her undies en route to the lodging.

She shouted out his name, and her pussy fixed around him.

"Ok, fuck!" he snarled, then, at that point, snorted and called out to out her as he detonated inside her.

"Indeed," she murmured with a murmur, then, at that point, was sleeping soundly.

"Lyvia?" he murmured, then, at that point, laughed.

He folded his arms over her and trusted that his bunch will release then, at that point, acknowledged at that point that in case she never gave him a solitary offspring, he would be glad to simply go through his time on earth with her.

Fucking until they nodded off; and adoring every second they were together.

~□~

"Lyvia!" Sharissa hollered as she wobbled to her companion when they strolled in the entryway.

"Shar!" Lyvia said with energy as she accepted her companion, then, at that point, remained back and shook her head. "See you, that is no joke."

Shar smiled. "Five and a half more weeks," she said, scouring her huge stomach.

"Do you know what it is yet?"

Shar shook her head. "We need to be astonished. Along these lines, we painted the nursery in blues and pinks just to be certain we covered everything."

Lyvia laughed, "sounds wonderful."

"It is," Shar said with unadulterated energy as she grabbed hold of Lyvia's hand, "come see."

Lyvia laughed as her companion hauled her through the house, to the nursery.

Raj and Dustin strolled into the house and found both their mates missing.

"Lyvia?" Raj called out.

Dustin laughed, "Sharissa is likely appearance her the nursery."

Raj grinned, "she should be gigantic at this point."

Dustin smiled, "goodness better believe it. Furthermore she's more lovely than any lady in the world."

Raj gestured, "I wish Lyvia, and I could have an offspring. Be that as it may, it appears to be the Goddesses have decided not to favor us."

Dustin carried his companion. "It might in any case occur."

Raj shrugged as he sat on the rear of the lounge chair. "Perhaps. In any case, if not,

I am glad to carry on with my life, just me and my mate."

Dustin gestured, "expressed like a genuine Fated Mate. Have you all said the L word at this point?"

Raj smiled, "that's right, more than a month prior."

"Great," Dustin said with a gesture, "since that is all you truly need. Your mate's affection. Offspring are only a reward."

"Did you simply consider our offspring a reward?"

Raj and Dustin went to their mates, and Dustin's cheeks became a striking shade of red.

"A reward close to you, Mafilia. We were examining that we would be cheerful assuming we just had our mates in our lives. That whelps are only a reward close to our delightful mates."
"Pleasant save," Raj murmured.

Dustin smiled, "in every case great to make a save with reality."

Shar smiled and strolled over to Dustin. "However long you don't let our whelps know that."

Dustin gestured and maneuvered his mate into his arms. "It's between us," he said then kissed her.

Lyvia checked out Raj, and Raj felt his heart skirt a thump.

"Is that how you truly feel?" she asked as she moved towards him. "You can live with it simply being both of us?"

Raj gestured, "Indeed, Mafilia. You are my Fated Mate; you are all I really want. I will adore any offspring you give me, yet on the off chance that I just have you, I will in any case be the most joyful Tiger on the planet."

She smiled as she folded her arms over his neck. "You're all I want as well."

He grinned and set his hands on her hips. "You sure? You're not discouraged any longer?"

She shrugged, "I will consistently be tragic that I can't give you the offspring you merit. Yet, I went to an acknowledgment while in my cloudiness. I love you and need you, and I will be glad assuming it's just you and me generally and until the end of time."

He smiled. "Sounds great to me," he said then kissed her.

The doorbell rang, and everybody went to the entryway.

"Who could that be?" Shar inquired.

Dustin moved over to the entryway and opened it.

"Gracious, hi, you should be Dustin," a natural voice said from the opposite side of the entryway.

Lyvia moved out of Raj's arms and strolled over to the way to observe a smiling Pearl on the opposite side.

"Pearl," Lyvia said, stunned to see the Witch.

"Lyvia, so great to see you once more," Pearl said with a brilliant grin.

"Dustin, this is a, uh... "

"Companion," Pearl said cheerfully. "I'm Pearl Owens, and you should be Dustin Kraftman, mate to... " She glanced around Dustin and recognized the extremely pregnant Sharissa. "Mated to the exquisite Human Sharissa Flemmings."

"What the hell?" Dustin said as he gazed at the lady then, at that point, taken a gander at Lyvia then Raj. "How did you respond? Tell her beginning and end, about everybody you know?"

"God help us," Pearl said before the other two could reply. "We just talked for a couple of moments, not sufficient opportunity to learn anything. I have had some significant awareness of both of you for a long time. In reality, every one of you four, yet that is irrelevant. I came to converse with Lyvia and Raj."

"You... What?" Dustin asked, befuddled.

Pearl grinned as she pushed past the confounded Shifter.

"Pearl is a... " Lyvia began to say yet couldn't wrap up.

"A Witch," Pearl said as though it was something regular to track down a Witch in your home.

"A what!?" Dustin cried as he moved to remain between the Witch and his mate.

Pearl waved her hand at him. "Relax, Shifter, I won't hurt your mate or your whelp. I'm a White Witch. Also, I came to talk with Lyvia and Raj about their fledglings."

"What whelps?" Lyvia asked with a screech.

"Goodness right, too early," Pearl said as she smacked herself in the brow with her palm.

"What's happening, Witch?" Raj requested as he stood up from the rear of the love seat.

Pearl grinned at them. "Kindly pull up a chair," she said as she motioned to the sofa, then, at that point, turned and checked out Shar and Dustin. "You as well. You play a major part to play in this also. Presently come sit."

Shar took a gander at Dustin, who was all the while frowning at Pearl.

"She said White Witch," she murmured to her mate.

She has perused many books since she tracked down her mate. Furthermore one of them was for sure on the Witches and which ones to trust. Also how to tell which ones are great. She pulled on Dustin's arm and murmured into his ear. He took a gander at her with wide eyes, then, at that point, vanished into the kitchen and returned with a jug of blanch.

"What the heck are you doing?" Lyvia shrieked when she saw Shar with the sanitizer.

Pearl gazed toward Shar as quiet as anyone might imagine and watched the Human poor the sanitizer over her arm.

"I realized you were the brilliant one," Pearl said happily.

"She's a White Witch okay," Shar said, then, at that point, begun hacking.

"Damn it, Shar, that was moronic. Fade exhaust can hurt you and the fledgling," Lyvia said as she moved over to her companion.

Dustin grabbed the container of fade from his mate and covered it, then, at that point, thrown it out the entryway.

"Try not to worry," Pearl said cheerfully, then, at that point, snapped the fingers of her right hand, and the air cleared, remembering the air for Shar's lungs, and the fluid on Pearl's arm dried in a split second. "No mischief done," she said cheerfully.

Dustin maneuvered Shar into his arms. "For what reason didn't you let me know the sanitizer could hurt you or our fledgling?"

Shar shook in her mate's arms, actually frightened that she hurt their whelp with her idiocy.

"I-I didn't have a clue," she cried against him.

"Shar, come here," Pearl said as she twisted her finger for her to move over to her.

Dustin remained nearby his mate as they strolled over to the Witch.

Pearl laid her hand over Shar's stomach and grinned. "Would you like to know the sex?"

"No," Shar and Dustin said simultaneously.

"We need to be amazed," Shar said happily.

Pearl gestured. "Your offspring is okay. The exhaust didn't make it past your lungs. Your lungs are spotless and clear. Might you want to hear the heartbeat?"

"Indeed," the mates said simultaneously, then, at that point, chuckled.

Pearl muttered something, then, at that point, a heartbeat reverberated in the room. "Extremely impressive heartbeat," Pearl said happily.

"That... that is our fledgling?" Shar asked, astounded at what they were hearing.

"Indeed," Pearl said cheerfully.

Dustin smiled as he pulled his mate's back against his chest.

"I will bring you something next opportunity I drop by, so you can hear your fledgling at whatever point you need," Pearl said, then, at that point, snapped her fingers, and the heartbeat halted.

"Much obliged to you," Shar said with tears in her eyes.

Pearl grinned, "you are generally welcome."

"I need to know why Shar poured dye on Pearl," Raj said, looking where Shar had poured the sanitizer on Pearl's arm.

"Since, supposing that she was a Dark Witch, her skin would have gurgled and rankled, and she'd have killed me... " Shar's eyes opened wide. She'd nearly gotten herself killed, ah crap.

"Killed you?" Dustin said with a snarl.

Pearl took a gander at them and grinned. "I figure a Dark Witch would have underhanded you, Shar, yet she wouldn't have killed you. You're a Fated Mate, which is against all laws of killing. In case she killed you, she'd need to manage the rage of the Goddesses. Slapping you, she'd have managed the Shifters and would have left before they could detach her head."

Dustin protested as he pulled his mate considerably nearer.

"Sorry," Shar murmured as she gazed toward her mate.

Chapter 10

Dustin didn't react to his mate's conciliatory sentiment, yet he held her nearer and let her know with his eyes that she's not escaping this with such ease.

Which drove her grin in light of the fact that mad sex is consistently hot!

"However, enough of that, how about we hit you up two," Pearl said as she went to Lyvia and Raj.

"What did you mean by offspring?" Lyvia asked as she got back to her put on the love seat.

"Indeed, I have been getting dreams of the Fated Mates for many years at this point. At the point when Dustin and Sharissa saw as one another, I got a fantasy of their whelp. Furthermore realized they'd observed one to be another."

"Are our youngsters significant?" Shar inquired.

Pearl grinned at her. "Vital to the fate of us all."

"Who is we all?" Dustin inquired.

"The Supernaturals, obviously," Pearl said cheerfully.

"I'm not a Supernatural, I'm a Human," Shar contended.

Pearl turned her head and grinned at her. "You are a Supernatural. You are a Fated Mate. Do you not have gifts past Human capacities?"

Shar gestured, "I have my matc's capacities."

"Everything except moving, yes," Pearl said with a gesture.

"I'm a Supernatural?" Shar asked with wide eyes and fervor in her voice.

"Without a doubt," Pearl said with a laugh. "So back to why I'm here," she said as she turned around to Lyvia and Raj. "Lyvia, I realize you have been worried about having your mate's whelp."

Lyvia gestured, "indeed, we have attempted and attempted," she said with a scowl.

Pearl grinned, "yet as I told you, it wasn't your time."

"What does that mean?" Dustin inquired.

Pearl glanced back at Dustin then at Lyvia and Raj once more. "Both of you were great many miles from home. Raj was playing a mind-blowing rounds. Furthermore you were there with him. Obviously you were unable to remain at home, and voyaging while at the same time conveying fledglings isn't protected."

"Fledglings?" Lyvia asked, her voice squeaking.

"Indeed," Pearl said, energy in her voice. "I envisioned with regards to them. Furthermore goodness, young lady, they're so excellent." She went to Shar and grinned at her. "So are yours."

"Do I have more than this one?" Shar asked as she put her hand over her stomach.

Pearl gestured, "indeed, you and your mate have mutiple. Yet, it's this pregnancy that is significant," she said happily. "Your whelp will lead them all."

"Ou-our whelp?" Shar squeaked.

Pearl laughed, "yours is the most established all things considered."

"The number of others?" Raj inquired.

Pearl took a gander at him. "A few more Fated Matcs and each couple will create the following stage to the military... "

"Armed force!" Shar almost shouted.

"Not the thoughtful you think," Pearl said, "your kids are bound to save the world. For what reason do you think the Goddesses made Fated Mates? They know when they will be required. That is the reason there haven't been any in such countless years."

"Wasn't Tate's folks the last?" Dustin inquired.

"Indeed," Pearl said.

"Yet, there was no conflict going on when Tate was conceived," Raj said. "There hasn't been in millennia. Not since... "

"Not since Christ, indeed, I know," Pearl said with a gesture. "Tate has an alternate destiny available for him."

"An alternate destiny?" Dustin asked, confounded.

Pearl gestured, "for one aiding you and your mates. Assuming you will see, he has a weakness for Fated Mates. Also his folks are an integral justification for that. Yet additionally, it was naturally introduced to him to ensure the Fated Mates."

"He's a protector, in a manner of speaking," Raj said with a gesture.

"In a manner of speaking," Pearl said with a gesture, "yet he likewise has another position. Yet, I can't uncover it to you, it's too early."

"Damn, this crap is confounding," Dustin said as he imploded into a seat then, at that point, maneuvered Shar onto his lap.

"What's going on that the Goddesses made us for?" Lyvia inquired.

"We won't know until the Goddesses feel fit to tell us," Pearl said. "At the point when I know, I will make certain to tell every one of you."

"Shouldn't something be said about our fledglings?" Raj inquired.

"Indeed, your fledglings," Pearl said cheerfully, "the Goddesses realized you weren't prepared. In this way, they hindered your origination while you were away. Yet, presently... " She said, pointing at Lyvia's stomach.

Lyvia folded her arms over her stomach. "No chance," she said, her eyes huge as saucers. "Sacred fuck."

"However, she just began her hotness yesterday," Raj said, then, at that point, looked from his mate to the Witch and back once more.

Pearl laughed. "What's more have you not saw how much more settled she is presently, after your first tryst the previous evening?"

Raj smiled from one ear to another. "Simply the once that is all it took?"

Pearl laughed, "that is everything necessary. Did it not just take once for Dustin and Shar once she quit taking her conception prevention?"

Dustin and Shar gestured.

"We're really going to have an offspring?" Lyvia screeched with satisfaction.

Raj held her nearby and kissed her sanctuary.

"No, Lyvia, you're not having a fledgling," Pearl said.

Lyvia's face fell. "Yet, you said... "

Pearl grabbed hold of her hand and crushed it. "Lyvia, you're the most uncommon of the gathering."

Lyvia's eyes squinted. "In what capacity?"

Pearl saw Raj then back at Lyvia. "Lyvia, what amount do you are familiar your family's past?"
Lyvia shrugged, "very little. They never truly preferred me since I was a young lady. My father just needed young men."

Pearl gestured, "that is on the grounds that the females on your father's side of the family have a high shot at being what their precursors were."

"I don't comprehend," Lyvia said with a shake of her head.

"Lyvia," Pearl said as she hurried nearer to her, "that is no joke."

Lyvia's eyes became wide, and her mouth fell open.

"Heavenly fuck," Raj said as he hopped back from his mate.

Dustin gazed at Lyvia from the seat as though she'd grown a subsequent head, and Shar gazed at everybody as though they'd all gone frantic.

"I-I can't be," Lyvia cried, "no," she said with a shake of her head.

"What's an Omega, and for what reason is Raj viewing at Lyvia as though she's an unfamiliar item?" Shar asked, watching her companions as they went ballistic.

"An Omega is an uncommon female Shifter that can convey more than each whelp in turn like a real creature. They're uncommon, and nobody has seen one of every many years," Dustin said, as yet gazing at Lyvia.

Lyvia began crying.

"Raj," Pearl said as she highlighted Lyvia.

Raj shook his head. What the heck is off-base with him? What a dick he is for bouncing away from his mate. So what, assuming she can have an entire litter of offspring on the double. She is his, and the offspring are theirs. He will cherish them all until the cows come home.

He moved his legs to one or the other side of his mate, then, at that point, pulled her back against his chest and held her.

"I love you, Lyvia," he murmured into her ear.

"Despite the fact that I'm an Omega?" she asked, as yet crying.

He laughed, "particularly in light of the fact that you're an Omega. Darling, that simply implies more children... "

"Ohmigod!" Lyvia shouted out. "How will we manage such countless whelps without a moment's delay?"

"That is the reason you are beginning The Fated Mates Club," Pearl said cheerfully.

"You are familiar that?" Shar asked as she sat ahead. Then, at that point, she contemplated that and leaned against her mate. "Obviously you do."

"You have companions to help you," Pearl said as she tapped Lyvia's hand.

"How... the number of?" Lyvia inquired.

Pearl grinned. "Four. Would you like to know the genders?"

Lyvia gestured then gazed toward Raj. "Isn't that right?"

Raj smiled, "sure."

"Three young men and a young lady," Pearl said, then, at that point, pressed Lyvia's hand when she began to hyperventilate. "After they're conceived, you go on the pill assuming that is any assistance."

Lyvia chuckled, "sounds great to me. We'll delay until they're out of the house before we attempt once more."

Raj laughed as he kissed her cheek.

"Indeed, I should get going now," Pearl said as she leaped to her feet.

"Remain for lunch?" Shar asked as she got to her feet.

"Wish I could," Pearl said cheerfully. "However, individuals are going thusly, and I can't meet them. It's not our fate to meet yet," she said, then, at that point, pulled a couple of shades from her satchel and set them on her nose. "Assuming you have any inquiries or at any point need me, call me." Cards showed up in their grasp. "Be careful," she said, then, at that point, surged out the entryway.

Pearl immediately strolled down the way towards the carport as four Shifters strolled up. She tried not to view at them as she rushed past them. Pearl detected one of them pause and view at her as she advanced toward her vehicle. If by some stroke of good luck she hadn't driven here, then, at that point, she could have poofed out of here before they arrived.

"Hello!" he hollered after her. "Don't I know you?!"

Pearl shut her eyes and opened her vehicle without utilizing her keys. She got into her vehicle as quick as possible and sped out of the carport without responding to him. She watched him in her rearview reflect. He shrugged, then, at that point, turned and strolled up the way to the entryway.

She took a full breath to quiet her nerves. "It's not our time yet, my adoration." She murmured, then, at that point, focused out and about as she made a beeline for her next stop.
"In this way, what do you genuinely think regarding what I am?" Lyvia asked Raj sometime thereafter as they prepared for bed.

Symone and Tiger were settled once more into her home, and Angel was with Shar. While she was gone, the cats had proceeded to grow up. She would rather not miss anything like that once more. Be that as it may, she will not request that Raj quit what he adores.

"I'm cheerful, Lyvia."

She went to him. "You're glad that I'm having not one, not two, not three but rather four whelps?"

He laughed, "Lyvia. They're a piece of you and a piece of me. I would be glad assuming you were having eight offspring."

She snorted, "no, you wouldn't. Yet, decent attempt."

He snarled as he hopped on the bed and pulled her down with him.

She snickered, and he kissed her.

"Lyvia. I love you. Furthermore I love our four little Tigers," he said, scouring her stomach. "You and I were bound to have these fledglings. Did you not hear what Pearl said?"

She grinned as she pushed a lock of hair behind his ear. "I love you as well. Yet, four?"

He smiled, "whatever the Goddesses need them for. They will be a fearsome group."

She snickered. "Group, huh? Is it accurate to say that you are searching for a Hockey group?"

He shook his head. "I'm setting Hockey aside for later for the time being."

She wheezed, "don't do that... "

He kissed her to quietness her. "It's now finished. I called before... "

"Gracious, Raj. Call them, let them know you've altered your perspective... "

"Lyvia. You can't travel while pregnant, particularly with four. Furthermore you realize we can't be isolated. It's just for a little while, perhaps three."

She began to cry, and he pulled her against him.

"It is my decision Lyvia. When the fledglings are mature enough to go with us, I'll reconsider Hockey. Also, dislike I'll be too old in ten or twenty years to begin playing once more. Also perhaps our young men or even our girl will get the game."

She snickered, "pleasant save there."

He laughed, "I would be glad in case our Tigress favored games like her dad."

She grinned, "I love you to such an extent."

He kissed her hard and profound. At the point when he surfaced for oxygen, they were both breathing vigorously.

"I love you more than my own life, and I will give you and our offspring all that I have."

She grinned up at him as she tenderly ran her fingertips down his jaw.

"All we require: is your affection."

Chapter 11

Sharissa set the skillet on the counter and grinned. She's been having the most odd longings. She checked out the brownies that were loaded up with peanut butter and strawberry jam. Alright, so not the best mix, but rather fuck, she needed a piece of it. She cut into it and lifted a piece, consuming her fingertips.

"Damn it," she cried as she dropped the square of brownie. The gooey focus overflowed over the highest point of different brownies, and her eyes lit up. "Great!" she shrieked.

She was spreading the strawberry jam over the (indeed ideal skillet of brownies) when Dustin strolled into the kitchen. He halted and gazed at the skillet.

"What on earth did you prepare this time?"

His voice made them bounce. She pivoted and smiled at her mate, the margarine blade she'd been utilizing to spread the jam in her grasp, which had naturally come up with good reason. The jam slid down her fingers, yet she didn't see as she gazed into her mate's eyes. She is so infatuated with this man, her Shifter.

Dustin smiled when he saw the vibe of unadulterated desire in his mate's eyes. He likewise saw love and his heart expanded. Dustin strolled over to her and grasped her hand into his. She kept on gazing at him as he pulled her hand to him and sucked one of her jam covered fingers into his mouth. He groaned, and she shuddered.

At the point when he let her finger go, her cheeks were nearly pretty much as red as the jam actually trickling from the blade.

Dustin smiled as he brushed his finger against her hot cheek. "Strawberry jam, my top pick."

She grinned as she inclined her cheek into his touch.

He took a gander at the container again and shook his head. "What have you prepared this time?"

Shar shook her head and cleared her considerations. "Peanut butter and jam brownies."

Dustin stifled out a chuckle. Her odd longings have given them a lot of weird new things to test.

"You don't get any," she said, pointing the blade at him, "assuming you chuckle at me."

He checked out her and shook his head. "I'm not snickering at you, Mafilia. I'm snickering at your odd longings."

She grunted. "Same thing," she said, then, at that point, returned to spreading the jam across the brownies.

When she was through, she lifted one out and took a chomp. She shut her eyes with a murmur.

"Great?" he asked, watching her.

She woke up and gestured. "Best thing I've concocted," she said, then, at that point, offered him a nibble.

Dustin smiled as he inclined forward and took a chomp. He bit it briefly, the flavors battling in his mouth for predominance. It really wasn't really awful.

"So?" Shar asked, watching him bite the chomp of brownie.

Dustin grinned, "better than the fish lasagna, however not generally so great as the pumpkin meringue pie."

Shar smiled, then, at that point, took one more nibble of the brownie. He hadn't enjoyed her lasagna. She'd needed to eat it all herself, not that she griped.

"Mother is coming over today," Dustin said as he inclined his hip against the counter.

Shar took a gander at him then at herself. "When?"

He checked the time. "In with regards to 60 minutes."

Shar's eyes opened in amazement. "I'm a wreck!"

Dustin laughed, "I don't figure she will mind."

Shar snorted as she pushed the remainder of the brownie into her mouth. "Set that aside for me," she said through the chocolaty goodness in her mouth, highlighting the skillet of brownies.

Dustin smiled as he watched his mate run from the kitchen. They have a lot of staff who could fix her anything she needed, however when they wouldn't make a portion of the dishes she longed for, she began making them herself. He didn't fault his staff. A portion of the things she has requested would make anybody run for the slopes. All with the exception of his excellent mate. He moaned as he lifted the skillet of brownies and set them into the refrigerator.

He realizes she will have them completed before tomorrow. She was getting a Shifter's hunger with the pregnancy. He laughed when he thought about a day or two ago when they were tossed from one more everything you can eat buffet. His little pregnant mate had wiped them out of nearly everything in under 60 minutes.

"Do you want anything, Mr. Kraftman?"

Dustin went to the house keeper and grinned. "Would you be able to please tidy up after my mate?"

The lady grinned and gestured, glad to have something to do. Since the time Shar moved in, there was less and less for his staff to do, on the grounds that Shar can be a slick oddity.

He had contemplated releasing his staff, however they're all Shifters who need work, and with Sharissa pregnant, they could utilize the assistance. They avoid sight and out of brain. Which Dustin appreciated, yet they realized they were there in light of the fact that the house remained clean. Fortunately, they have consistently given him his space, or he and Shar would have been gotten at least a time or two fucking in some room in his manor.

The doorbell rang, and he hurried out of the kitchen to answer the entryway. At the point when he opened the entryway, his mom remained on the opposite side, radiating at him. She hurled herself entirely into his arms, and he laughed as he embraced her.

"That is no joke."

Amirah Kraftman grinned as she embraced her subsequent oldest. "I was unable to hold back to see you and your wonderful mate."

Dustin laughed. He realizes the reason why she's here. Since Shar is pregnant with her first grandcub.

"Where is she?" Amirah asked as she moved past her child and into his enormous chateau.

"Cleaning up. She was somewhat of a wreck subsequent to making one more of her creations."

Amirah went to her child with a laugh. "Is it true that she is at the insane yearnings stage?"

Dustin laughed as he gestured. "She is."

"What did she compose today?" Amirah asked as she strolled over to a sofa and plunked down.

"Peanut butter and jam brownies."

Amirah's left eyebrow raised. "Inside or on top?"

"Both," Dustin laughed, "peanut butter and strawberry jam inside and jam over the top."

Amirah gestured, "I hadn't put jam on top. I covered it with peanut butter."

Dustin gazed at her, his mouth expanding open.

Amirah laughed, "your offspring has similar longings you did when I was pregnant with you."

Dustin's mouth shut, and a smile spread across his face.

"Amirah," Shar screeched when she strolled into the family room and observed Amirah sitting on the lounge chair conversing with Dustin.

Amirah gazed toward Shar and grinned. "You look totally perfect."

Shar become flushed. She realizes she doesn't. Her hair is wet and lying straight down her back, and her garments are adhering to her clammy skin.

Amirah strolled over to Sharissa and maneuvered her into an embrace. "Parenthood looks heavenly on you."

Shar grinned as she embraced the lady back.

Amirah remained for a couple of hours. She told Shar accounts of when she was pregnant with every one of her children, particularly Dustin. She had lunch with them and sat out back while they talked about the jungle gym Dustin needed to work in the lawn. At the point when it was the ideal opportunity for her to go, Shar was pitiful for her to leave.

"I will come for another visit, I guarantee," Amirah said with a smile. "What's more I will see you this end of the week for family night. You're not missing another," she said as she went to her child and gave him the stink eye.

They hadn't been to a family supper since they'd found Shar was pregnant.

"Guarantee," Shar said with a smile.

Amirah gestured then highlighted Shar's stomach. "Deal with my grandcub."

Shar gestured, "rely on it."

Amirah smiled, "I will give you the plans I thought of while pregnant with Dustin. It appears to be your fledgling has its dad's craving."

Shar laughed, "I'd love that."

Amirah embraced them then went out.

Shar took a gander at Dustin. "What's the deal?"

Dustin smiled. "Room," he said, then, at that point, lifted her into his arms and conveyed her up the steps.

Shar laughed as she clutched him.

~□~

Shar was in the kitchen going through the cookbook Amirah had given her at the family supper the previous evening when she heard a boisterous commotion outback. She put the book down and strolled towards the entryway.

An uproarious snarl and a murmur made them pull the entryway open. She observed Symone floating over her cats as she murmured and smacked at a difficult canine to get to the little ones.

Shar strolled down the steps quicker then she ought to have and halted when the canine gazed toward her with a wild snarl.

"Insidious mutt," Shar snarled at the canine.

With the canine occupied with Shar, Symone hopped onto the canine's head, murmuring and pawing.

Shar saw the blood trickling into the canine's eye and nearly shouted when the canine shook his head, throwing Symone across the yard.

"Symone!" Shar shouted out. She headed towards the feline, however the canine went to her and snarled, froth trickling from his mouth. "Ok fuck," she murmured.

The little cats yowled and hurried over to Shar. As though they realized she would ensure them while their mom was down.

"Escape my yard," Shar snarled at the mut.

The frothing mutt moved towards her and halted when Shar hunched in a cautious position and growled at the canine. The canine growled back and shook his head, spit flying all over the place. He moved to seize her and halted with a little cry.

Obscure to Shar, and concealed by anybody, her eyes streaked silver briefly.

The mutt snarled and seized her once more. Shar ready for the aggravation however was stunned when a Wolf appeared suddenly and brought the mutt down. She watched the Wolf grab hold of the mutt's neck and shake his head. She heard the snap of the mutt's neck and set her hand to her throat as she remained from her guarded hunch.

The Wolf went to her, and she could see the generosity in his silver eyes. He moved to his Human structure, and Shar murmured with alleviation. It was Dustin's grounds-keeper.

"I'm sorry I didn't arrive sooner, ma'am," he said with a slight bow of his head.

Shar grinned, "you arrived without a moment to spare, Fredrick."

Fredrick smiled, "you know my name."

Shar gestured, and before she could say whatever else, Dustin burst from the house and halted at the highest point of the steps taking in everything in his lawn.

"Fredrick?" he asked his landscaper.

"It's my issue," Shar said, grinning up at her mate.

Dustin checked out Sharissa, his left eyebrow raised.

"I will deal with this," Fredrick said, then, at that point, gotten the dead mutt and strolled into the forest to cover him.

The little cats mewing grabbed Shar's eye, and she recollected Symone. She raced to the feline, who was all the while lying on her side, not moving.

"Gracious, Symone, if it's not too much trouble, be alright. Lyvia won't ever pardon me," Shar cried.

Dustin followed his mate and the cats to where the mother feline laid unmoving.

"What occurred?" he asked as he remained behind her.

Shar moved the feline and murmured with alleviation. She was as yet alive. In any case, would she say she was alright?

"We should take Symone to the vet," she said as she lifted the feline into her arms.

Dustin glared. "What occurred, Sharissa?"

Shar saw her mate and scowled, then, at that point, told him everything.

Dustin moaned. "Remind me to give Fredrick a raise," he said, then, at that point, folded his arms over her and strolled her to the house.

They arranged the cats in a room then, at that point, made a beeline for the vehicle to take Symone to the vet.

The vet provided Symone with a doctor's approval. She had a couple of injuries, however nothing was broken. At the point when they returned home, they set Symone in the room with her infants then, at that point, made a beeline for their room.

"Presently for your discipline," Dustin snarled as he strolled up behind his mate.

Shar turned on him, her eyes open wide. "You wouldn't dare."

He scowled, "Sharissa. You nearly got yourself and our offspring killed."

Shar scowled, "I was ensuring Symone and her children."

Dustin murmured, "their lives aren't a higher priority than you or our whelp."

Shar's scowl developed. "They aren't any less significant, by the same token."

Dustin snarled, "Sharissa."

"Dustin."

Dustin squeezed the extension of his nose. "What discipline would it be advisable for me to give you for your carelessness?"

Shar shrugged, "I didn't realize he had rabies until after I joined Symone and her cats."

Dustin moaned, "precisely. Wildness."

Shar peered down at her stomach. He was correct. She shouldn't have bounced in like that without knowing what she was getting into.

Dustin maneuvered her into his arms. "Your discipline will be torment."

She gazed up at him, her eyes open wide. "'I'-t-torment?"

He smiled, "relax, Mafilia, it will hurt me however much it will hurt you."

She flickered. How the screw will her torment hurt him?

She discovered that evening. Each time she was going to climax, Dustin would move in an opposite direction from her pussy. Then, at that point, he would go at it once more, carrying her to a limit, then, at that point, delivering her before she could cum. He did it for a really long time, and she was going to submit murder.

She could recognize easily that it was to be sure harming him however much it was harming her. What's more she smiled.

Following three hours of torment, Dustin at last had enough of the torture and figured it was sufficient discipline. He let her climax then, at that point, rammed into her so hard she shouted. He smiled as he banged into her over and over. The strain from not letting his mate climax was a lot for him. He came so hard that assuming she wasn't at that point pregnant, he realized she would be currently.

"What the hell was that?" Sharissa shouted out.

Dustin grunted, "I don't think this was a decent discipline."

She laughed. "Why? Since you were rebuffed too?"

He snorted. "Since I don't think it has shown you something new to act."

She moaned, "indeed, that was the best sex we've at any point had. Possibly I'll be awful more frequently."

Dustin laughed, "I love you."

Shar smiled, "I love you as well, Mafilio. Beyond what words might at any point say."

He smiled. "Indeed, even after your discipline?"

She laughed, "the delayed consequences were great."

He shook his head. "You are one insane lady."

Her eyebrow raised. "Didn't you definitely realize that?"

He gestured, "tragically, I did. Since who else however an insane lady would with such ease give herself to a man like me?"

Shar put her hand to his cheek. "Our association might have been quick and insane as damnation. In any case, I wouldn't exchange it for anything. I love you, Dustin, and nothing will at any point change that. You are my other a large portion of, my perfect partner."

Dustin grinned, "and you are mine. Until further notice, and all time everlasting."

"The number of whelps do you need?" Shar asked all of a sudden.

Dustin checked out her, his eyebrow raised. "What number of do you need?"

She jeered, "I asked you first."

He smiled, "somewhere around four."

She grinned, "I believe we're an ideal match, Dustin Kraftman."

Dustin inclined down overall quite well (he was as yet tied inside her) and kissed the highest point of her stomach.

"You and our fledgling are my beginning and end, Sharissa. I love you both to such an extent."

Shar grinned. "Also we love you," she said as she slid her fingers through his hair. "Regardless of whether the Goddesses hadn't tossed us together, I think we'd have observed each to be other somehow."

He laughed, "you came to us to assist you with moving away from your insane ex."

She gestured and shut her eyes. In case that man hadn't referenced the Kraftman siblings, she couldn't ever have considered them... Was that the

Goddesses' method of tossing them together?

Dustin's rooster made a commotion when it jumped out of her, and she snickered.

Dustin laughed as he moved to the top of the bed and set down. He pulled her against him and moaned vigorously.

"Much obliged to you," Shar murmured.

Dustin squeezed his cheek to her head. "For what?"

"For being you," she murmured, then, at that point, nodded off.

Dustin moaned. "No, Mafilia," he said, then, at that point, kissed her temple, "much obliged."

Chapter 12

Josie Potter did not know how she endure the mishap, or why she was directed to a Shifter Bar. All she knows is she's drained and frightened. In any case, the Shifters who help her, are thoughtful and one of them professes to be her mate.

What's the significance here, in any case?

Presently she's secured an office with her... mate... She can't avoid the draw to him, and what occurs next is past her creative mind. However at that point their decent world they'd made together, is pulled separated, in a real sense.

She didn't anticipate being in the emergency clinic subsequent to having the best sex of her life, however there she sat, her mate in the bed close to hers. What a beginning to her new existence with The Fated Mates Club.